Praise for *The Invisible Promise*

"Since the turn of the century, market power has been shifting from the vendor to the customer, and offer power from products to services. Marketing services in a customer-centric world is at the core of the new economy, and Harry Beckwith is the best guide you could have as you navigate these new waters."

—Geoffrey Moore, Author, *Crossing the Chasm*
and *Zone to Win*

"Harry Beckwith is not just one of my favorite thinkers about branding and service marketing; he's one of my favorite writers. His tight, clean, storytelling prose drives forward to key insights to improve your business."

—David Gardner, Founder and CEO, *The Motley Fool*

"For twenty-five years, Harry Beckwith has seen what we cannot and then turned what is 'invisible' to us into a vision. He has done it again with *The Invisible Promise*."

—Ty M. Votaw, former Commissioner,
Ladies Professional Golf Association

"My favorite sage on marketing has come up with this best yet. Harry's observations—short, powerful, and memorable—are incredibly inspiring. I devoured *The Invisible Promise* in one sitting, and leapt up to apply it."

—Derek Sivers, Entrepreneur and Author

"Our firm thrived by following Harry's insights, and *The Invisible Promise* will help you do the same. Through his wonderful stories, written with a clarity and wit that make the book so delightful to read, *The Invisible Promise* remains especially compelling in the new business era of internet and communications technology."

—Clifford Greene, Founding Partner, Greene Espel

"For more than two decades, I have devoured Harry's ideas on marketing the invisible—in software, music, finance, law, and consulting. The rise of online marketing and social media makes his ideas in *The Invisible Promise* even more important today. I already am applying them in my business and recommending them to everyone in my network."

—David Meerman Scott, best-selling Author of 12 books
including *The New Rules of Marketing and PR*

"When I read *Selling the Invisible*, I knew Harry Beckwith was both a winner and a sage. *The Invisible Promise* and Harry Beckwith have the process right side up. It's hard to find answers that make sense. It's hard to find answers that you can use the minute you read them. And it's almost impossible to find answers that work. This book answers all three questions both invisibly and visibly. Let me give you my best two words of advice: buy it!"

—**Jeffrey Gitomer, Author,** *Little Red Book of Selling*

THE INVISIBLE PROMISE

Also by Harry Beckwith

Selling the Invisible

You, Inc.

Unthinking

What Clients Love

The Invisible Touch

THE
INVISIBLE
PROMISE

*A Field Guide to Marketing
in an Upside-Down World*

HARRY BECKWITH

Matt Holt Books
An Imprint of BenBella Books, Inc.
Dallas, TX

Matt Holt is an imprint of BenBella Books, Inc.
10440 N. Central Expressway
Suite 800
Dallas, TX 75231
benbellabooks.com
Send feedback to feedback@benbellabooks.com

BenBella and *Matt Holt* are federally registered trademarks.

Printed in the United States of America
10 9 8 7 6 5 4 3 2 1

Library of Congress Control Number: 2022013518
ISBN 9781637741924 (hardcover)
ISBN 9781637741931 (electronic)

Editing by Katie Dickman
Copyediting by Michael Fedison
Proofreading by Isabelle Rubio and Ariel Fagiola
Indexing by WordCo Indexing Services, Inc.
Text design and composition by PerfecType, Nashville, TN
Cover design by Harry Beckwith
Printed by Lake Book Manufacturing

To David Macy-Beckwith

Contents

Introduction

You Are Not Selling Toothpaste or Teslas

In 1997, in *Selling the Invisible,* I pointed out that 75 percent of Americans worked in service companies and that by 2005, that figure would top 80 percent. But if you wanted to know how to market a service, there was little to be found. Searching *Harvard Business Review*'s compendium of marketing case studies, I found that only one in four dealt with services. We were a services economy, I realized, living with a product marketing model.

And this trend to service has accelerated. In 2000, seven of America's Fortune 10 companies were product manufacturers. Today, there is only one: Exxon.

We live in a nation dominated by services, but by a marketing model from the world of products, most famously from Procter & Gamble: features and benefits, Unique Selling Propositions, positioning. It's the world of the famous four Ps: product, price, place, and promotion.

But if you are responsible for marketing a service, you soon begin to wonder if those principles fit. And then you realize that they don't. You need to alter your approach radically.

And there is a good reason for this: a service is nothing at all like a product.

Start with the first P, product. A service is not a P at all. A product is tangible. Take a new car. You can see it, touch it, feel it. You even are seduced by its smell and its sounds: the nice roar of its engine, the famously satisfying thud of its closing car door. Often, you are delighted with products like that car—the perfect black dress, that new carbon fiber driver with the head the size of a waffle iron, the latest Air Jordans—before you even buy it. Products are immediately satisfying.

Now compare this to a service. At the time you agree to purchase a service, it is invisible to you. You buy your services touch-, taste-, feel-, smell-, and sight-unseen.

Now the second P, price. Products have price tags. Services usually do not. Instead, a representative of the service promises to "go back to work up an estimate." As a prospect at that moment, you are not sure you will be willing or able to pay the amount the service rep eventually quotes.

And if a product fails, you know it: your computer screen goes blank, the headphones go silent, your milk goes sour. But knowing when a service fails, or even if it has failed, is much harder. Are those wedding photographs you received as nice as the ones you were shown? Should your knee still be aching four weeks after surgery? And was that a good tax return? If you know enough to question a tax return an accountant does for you, you know enough to do it yourself.

And because product failures are obvious and provable, most products can be warrantied. Few services can be. As a result, your only recourse for most service failures is a long and painful negotiation or an even longer and more expensive litigation.

Even more critical today, in the last thirty years, we have lived through a quality revolution. Manufacturers make products using well-tested and computer-monitored processes that ensure ever more remarkable quality. As just one example, the word "lemon" for a bad car has disappeared from our vocabulary.

Service companies, by contrast, deliver their "products" through a series of acts that rarely can be routinized into a fail-safe process for producing a superior outcome. No one has devised a method, for example, for turning out consistently effective radio commercials.

And it is challenging to devise a service process, much less manage one. A client flies into town. The person in charge of the account takes him to dinner, downs three gin and tonics, and trips three times before reaching the exit. The client fires your firm the next day.

What "process" possibly could have prevented that costly service failure?

So, compared to products, services are loose cannons on decks, capable of breaking free and wreaking havoc aboard your ship at any moment. As the poor captain, you never feel in perfect control, and your poor prospect or client worries even more.

And there is another critical difference that affects how you design, distribute, and promote a service. The products you buy are made by people miles away, even continents away. So we rarely take product failures personally. But a service is provided to us by someone we have come to know. So, when a service fails us, we take it and often address it personally. "How could you do this to me?"

So, every day, as a service marketer—doctor or dog walker or dry cleaner—you face prospects sensitive to any mistake you might make, added cost you might charge, or any promise you may not keep.

And this is where service marketing, unlike product marketing, begins. It begins with a clear understanding of the salient traits of every service prospect: Fear, uncertainty, and doubt.

You must approach marketing a service differently. The four Ps either do not apply or apply in ways that are significantly different.

And positioning, features and benefits, Unique Selling Propositions? No, no, and no.

That is what this book is about—that, and the changes in our world, in the exactly twenty-five years since *Selling the Invisible* appeared, that have significantly altered how you market and deliver a service. Service marketing is different from product marketing, the 2020s are different from the 2000s, and my added twenty-five years of working with hundreds of services all over the world have added to, and in some cases altered, my understanding. This book tracks my new understanding of the service marketing sequence: planning your business; reaching and persuading your prospects; and finally, but light-years from least, relating to the clients you acquire.

PLANNING

An Upside-Down World

The Competition Challenge

Twenty years ago, big really mattered.

That's because prospects had limited access to information about companies and their services. So prospects chose, with remarkable frequency, the service with which they felt most familiar, thanks to its frequent advertising, and often the service with the biggest Yellow Pages ad.

Buyers naturally assumed a service successful enough to advertise must be pretty good, and the service with the biggest ad might be the best.

This meant that a company could buy a market. Today, it can't. Few prospects read newspapers and magazines, most aren't exposed to print ads, and most record their favorite television programs and skip over the commercials.

In short, the biggest barrier to entry in a market—having the resources to build your brand though advertising—has been all but eliminated.

When *Selling the Invisible* appeared, a professional-looking capabilities brochure cost at least $40,000. Few tiny businesses, and only trust-funded sole proprietors, could afford one. Now, a one-woman consultancy can look remarkably like Boston Consulting. She can hire a good designer and capable coder and put up a smart-looking website from an inexpensive template. The cost is approaching zero.

The result: Now the little can look like the big.

A famous 1993 *New Yorker* cartoon hinted at this. It showed a black dog seated in front of a computer keyboard and looking down at his spotted dog friend.

"On the internet," the black dog tells Spot, "no one knows you're a dog."

On the internet, a dog can appear to be a prince, and a one-man band can look like Maroon 5. It no longer costs much to look reputable, even excellent.

Everyone can get in the game.

The greater the competition, the more the need for distinction. Find yours.

The Quality Challenge

In 1959, Volkswagen unveiled the second ad of a campaign that an *Advertising Age* poll, forty years later, would name the greatest of all time. The headline, below a large photo of the little '59 Beetle, was just one word: "Lemon."

Americans often heard that word for an irreparably bad car. And it was true, because no one in the early decades of the twentieth century believed that factories could mass-produce products without some failures. The idea behind statistical quality control, the first major quality movement in America, actually was to tolerate defects, and merely reduce them to an acceptable minimum. As historian Daniel Boorstin noted in his Pulitzer Prize–winning book, *The Americans: The Democratic Experience*, "Products . . . were no better than they needed to be."

And then Japanese industry invaded America in the 1970s. They came with automobiles and electronics that seemed never to fail, and rarely did. Our standards went up and our economy began to suffer— badly. Seeing this, Congress stepped in and passed the Magnuson– Moss Warranty Act, which few people know by that name, but millions know by its popular name: the Lemon Law.

Six years later, Ford tried to assure car buyers that Ford was doing fine by launching a massive campaign, "At Ford, Quality Is Job One." Americans took some persuading; Ford had to run the campaign for seventeen years.

But eventually, the "New Quality Movement"—certain that products could be nearly perfect, rather than merely as good as they needed to be—worked. And that movement continues to bear fruit—other than lemons, of course. Products under any given brand name—Ford, Motorola, Crest—don't get worse over time; they get better. Their processes ensure it. So a product brand doubles as an assurance of quality.

But what about services? Totally controlled, refined, and monitored processes produce products, but most services come from a single, unmonitored human being. And to err is not only human; it's a daily event.

Your services come from people, not proven processes, and people come and go. When it's the stars that flee—the hot copywriter, the art director, the James Beard Award–winning chef, as three examples— the service's reputation suffers, even if it maintains the same high quality. There's no process in place to prevent that decline.

But the pressure is on. Great products have created great expectations for quality. We should all take to our hearts the message on a ten-yard-wide poster for Stanford University's football team:

"If you aren't getting better, you are getting worse. There is no staying the same."

Plan to get better—constantly.

The Disney Challenge

Your client's wife wins an incentive trip that takes her and her husband to a Four Seasons, where they arrive by limousine. For spring break, they explore Disney World and are catered to, Disney style.

Now that's service, her husband decides.

Back home the next day, he orders new Stan Smith tennis shoes from a store 1,800 miles away. The shoes arrive the next day.

Now *that's* service, he decides, just as you would.

And these realizations stick.

Those experiences become the man's standard of service excellence. It's not the standard in your industry; it's the standard in his mind. If I can get a chocolate under my pillow, a smile from every "cast member," a well-groomed man to hold my car door, and a package delivered in near real time, he decides, shouldn't I get your return phone call seconds after I hit "send"?

You study your industry, and you copy. But your industry may fail at serving clients. The printing industry is notorious for it. So are taxi services and collection agencies. Designers routinely rely on the excuse that their muse is late. ("We have some good ideas, but want to flush them out. Can you give us two more days?")

And now in the digital age, these weak industries find themselves in a bull's-eye, as ambitious twentysomethings see an imperfect industry and devise a new model to set the flawed one ablaze. So, goodbye taxicabs, hello Uber. Goodbye printers, hello Vistaprint. Goodbye designers awaiting their muses, hello Squarespace. Goodbye travel agents, hello Travelocity and Expedia.

Your industry doesn't establish the standards in your prospects' minds. *Your services do.* If you want ordinary clients, meet your industry's standards. But if you want delighted ones—the ones whose referrals and repeat business determine your long-term success—stop watching your competitors.

And start watching Disney, the Four Seasons, and FedEx instead.
You aren't competing with Dave. You are competing with Disney.

The Speed Challenge

When I was young, instant was bad.

Instant oatmeal tasted like library paste, instant chocolate milk tasted like sweetened chalk, and instant orange juice—Tang—tasted like cough medicine.

This famous cartoon hung on the walls of several thousand car repair shops, printers, and other service providers:

Sloth may have been among the Seven Deadly Sins, but life was slow.

And the internet didn't change that—at first. I vividly recall the searches I attempted in the months after I finished writing *Selling the Invisible*. After dinner, I'd launch the too-aptly-named WebCrawler. I'd enter my item, say "brands." (I couldn't do this during the day, not incidentally. Too many other people already were on WebCrawler's site.)

I'd stand up from my desk, wander to the kitchen, and build a sandwich. Then I'd trudge back to my Macintosh.

The search wasn't done. Or, just as often, the whole thing had crashed.

Occasionally, I got some results. But they'd be articles on cattle brands or something else unrelated to what I was looking for.

But on September 4, 1998, Sergey Brin and Larry Page started Google. And a year later, they launched. Search soon was nearly instant, and, unlike those instants of my childhood, instant was good and about to get better.

We are in the Age of Instant. On Twitter, we get the day's big headlines split seconds after the event occurs. We have something called, literally and appropriately, instant text messages, notifications on our phones, and predictive text and grammar/spelling suggestions in documents and emails.

Word processors eliminated the time of cutting, pasting, and slowly white-outing and then retyping our mistakes on printed paper.

Text messaging eliminated the time we took to click on our answering machines and listen to each of many wordy messages. And it reduced that wordiness because—again, to save our time—we text far fewer words than we speak.

Blogger eliminated the hours it took to set up a blog.

Facebook eliminated the time it takes to reach your friends. Now, you can reach them all at once. Twitter had the same effect and allowed you to reach friends in no more than 140 characters, a limit they doubled to 280 in 2017. (Tellingly, Twitter also recently cut its home "What is Twitter?" description from 30 to 16 words.)

Amazon eliminated the time of traveling to and from a bookstore and looking through its aisles for books and, often worse, learning the store didn't have a book in stock.

And Google eliminated the days it once took to research a topic— as every author knows, often just before nodding to the heavens and giving thanks.

And the faster we get things, the faster we want them. It's telling that we now regard the slower lanes of traffic as foolish; we call the fast one the "sane" lane.

You once had to poke your finger into a hole in a dial and then turn it to move that dial, and repeat that at least seven times, just to make a phone call. Now you push a single bar. Done.

Several years ago, Target CEO Robert Ulrich echoed the new mantra of the age, "Be quick or be gone." Ulrich said it was simple:

"Speed is life."

We are flying in hell-bent hurries, and thousands of businesses are satisfying our desire for it. If you are not among them, you are at risk.

But that also means you could be in luck. How can you thrive in our age of Speed Is Life?

What does your service cost your clients?

How can you reduce the cost of their time?

Can you go to them, instead of them to you?

Can you edit your advice so they can read and understand it faster?

Can you shrink your white papers, blogs, and case studies by 30 percent? (Yes, you can.)

Can you eliminate waiting time?

To make your service more attractive, look at every way to make it simpler and faster.

Plan to get faster. We want it right now.

The Major Challenge: America the Untrusting

According to recent studies, only one in three of us trusts teachers, only three in ten trust police officers, and fewer than three in ten of us trust scientific studies.

And while medicine is the most trusted service profession—half of us trust our primary doctor—even our trust in medicine is declining. In 1966, three in four of us expressed confidence in medical personnel. In 2019, only one in three of us did.

Whom do we trust? Major brands, actually. Their devotion to Six Sigma quality—the optimum possible—appears to have paid off: 74 percent of us say that the average major company will deliver consistently. But that figure drops significantly if you are not a major brand company, to just 55 percent. And according to the Edelman Trust Index, our trust in American businesses declined 5 percent over just the twelve months of 2016 alone.

But no one can equal us marketers for earning Americans' mistrust. A 2015 study commissioned by the American Association of Advertising Agencies revealed that only 26 percent of Americans believe that advertisers and marketers "practice integrity."

So, as soon as you begin to sound like a marketer, you begin to lose a prospect's trust.

Talk like a solution, not like a marketer.

Overvaluing the Medium, Undervaluing the Message

When I first set out to write this book, the wave of these All New! ideas had morphed into a tsunami. And then an event in a coffee shop a short walk from Minneapolis's Bde Maka Ska (previously named Lake Calhoun) changed my perspective.

Two young marketing consultants were telling me that I no longer should strive for succinctness and clarity in my writing. Instead, I needed to find ways to repeat three or four key phrases in each of my posts.

No synonyms; just repeat that key phrase. This tactic would "optimize my website."

"Won't it annoy my readers?" I asked

They shook their confident young heads. "Antiquated thinking."

Bewildered, I mentioned that Google was spending billions of dollars hiring brilliant engineers. Weren't these Silicon Valley wizards going to catch on to these tricks?

No, these experts told me. You're not writing for your readers and clients. You're writing for SEO—search engine optimization.

I couldn't resist. "Will it pay me $675 an hour?"

"Don't be ridiculous."

Miss, you took those words from my mouth.

That chat over coffee told me to fold my tent. I began writing a novel and waiting for this storm to pass.

It continued for a time. Every day I read about something that was going to change our clients' lives forever. Infographics—the Next New

Thing, along with the five reasons they were indispensable to your web-based marketing. (I am not kidding.)

But I felt sure these ideas were wrong because each began with a flawed assumption: that the medium mattered more than the message. Of what use is an infographic or an SEO-optimized website that has nothing compelling, credible, or persuasive to say? Of what use is a merely ordinary think piece, when readers have been exposed to so many excellent ones?

And what if your SEO drives people to your site to read an ordinary piece oddly stuffed with redundant "key phrases"? Or to a website that has been optimized for search engines but not for its persuasiveness?

What you need are not new or different vehicles for conveying your message but a truly compelling message.

Your medium is just a screen; your message is your movie.

The Bullshit Challenge

In the spring of 2007, a man whose identity I will protect decided there had to be some truth in all those promises of marketing gold.

So he hired a designer to create a new website, a writer to help him craft a weekly blog, and an SEO firm to optimize his site and blog.

Over lunch one November day in 2015, I asked this fellow how much he had spent on these services.

"North of $135,000."

"And how much of your time?"

"About six hours a week."

"Can you estimate your return on investment?"

He did not look up from his bowl of wild rice soup. "I'm not sure there has been any."

Once more: What matters is your message, not its medium.

The Bullshit Challenge: Advice from My Dad and the Ancient Romans

My late father was a surgeon who regularly dispensed excellent advice—along with far too many horrible puns—in memorable ways.

What I remember hearing most often was this: "Your logic is irrefutable, but your hypothesis is all wrong."

And my second favorite fatherly suggestion applies perfectly here.

"Well, Son—consider the source."

Invaluable advice today, considering that the internet has made it possible for everyone to pose as an authority.

And that's the problem. There are no barriers to entering the apparent authority market. There is no editor to put the publication's stamp of approval and reputation on the article. Worse, there is little to prevent the author from simply making things up.

Great magazines and newspapers still aspire to be "publications of record." Even *Us Weekly*, which reasonably can be called a gossip magazine, has a six-person fact-checking department. So does *Glamour*. And the *New Yorker*, credited with inventing the professional fact-checker by hiring Nancy Ford in 1923, has assembled a famously obsessive army of seventeen.

But no one vets blogs and most other articles posted on the internet; no one gives the authors their publication's endorsement; no one fact-checks them. And as you probably have discovered, perhaps painfully, many of these articles are not articles at all. They are advertisements for the person writing them, touting the superb service they are raving about.

The Romans were on to this. As early observers of hucksterism in sales, they coined the famous phrase *caveat emptor*: let the buyer beware.

Less famously, however, the Romans devised a similar phrase that is perfectly apt in this era of the Internet Authority:

Caveat lector. Let the reader beware.

Consider the marketing advice you read. Is it advice, or is it an advertisement?

Do You Believe in Miracles?

When Mark Zuckerberg of Facebook and Jack Dorsey of Twitter created these possible marketing vehicles—Facebook, Twitter, and others—they also created a massive number of services intent on proving that they could train you how to deploy them and grow your business.

This begat millions of new bloggers, thousands of SEO firms, half a dozen Social Media Gurus. This generation of geniuses assured you that your marketing problem wasn't your service or your message; it was your medium. Use these media wisely—"we will show you how"—and these vehicles—banner ads, Instagram pages, better landing pages—somehow were going to unleash years of pent-up demand for your services.

These articles—no doubt you read them and suffered from Fear of Missing Out, too—told you these new things were "changing marketing forever."

They didn't, of course. That's because the media used for marketing don't change marketing at all; they merely serve as vehicles for it.

Beware of miracles.

A Revelation at the Great Wall

My then eight-year-old son Cole and I were ascending the Great Wall of China behind a mass of tourists and an unusual number of young and tall Chinese women. Their preference for fashion over form could not have been more vivid: they were wearing five-inch heels (hence, the tall) and Gloria Vanderbilt and Calvin Klein jeans.

Fascinated about brands, I wondered if I had come upon the world's most brand-conscious people, the young Chinese.

I filed this away. I was in China, after all, to advise China Fashion Council. And the council needed someone's good advice; China fashion was not selling outside China. But even worse, it was not selling inside China, either. And there, staring at me from the back-right pockets of half-a-dozen American jeans, was the reason:

Fashion-conscious Chinese women bought branded products.

The country's fashion designers and manufacturers, however, had one enormous asset. Chinese silk was second to none and readily available at a cost far below what Gloria Vanderbilt and Calvin Klein and Giorgio Armani had to pay.

And China fashion had one other conspicuous asset. I saw it the instant I opened the brochure that the client had mailed to me in Minneapolis: the fashion had distinctive, understated, flattering design.

This was a revelation.

I added up all these elements—brand-consciousness, brilliant design, and beautiful silk at great prices—and had my answer for the council: they needed to go to Paris Fashion Week. Debut their fashions there, I would tell them, then work with the eager Chinese press to publicize China's debut at the fashion world's most famous event. Fashion-conscious women in Beijing and Shanghai would read of this historic debut in the fashion world and seek out these beautiful and brilliantly designed dresses and blouses. Of course!

I confidently offered this recommendation and rationale for it at a major conference in Beijing. I looked at my Chinese client and instantly recognized his expression. He was probably muttering to himself whatever is Chinese for "What on earth are you thinking, Harry?"

As so often happens in my business, I licked my wounds, and Cole and I, after another day of sightseeing, flew home.

Years passed—twelve, in fact—until one day when I picked up the *Wall Street Journal*. A smile on my face, I read the news: China's debut at Paris Fashion Week was the talk of the city. And this reminded me of the greatest plague in marketing:

Overconfidence in one's position.

My Chinese client had been confident for years about the future of fashion in China: all that he needed to do was persuade Chinese women of the quality and value of China fashion. People bought quality.

Well, many people do. But fashion-conscious Chinese women still bought brands—and brands, in his view, were frivolous. And it had cost his industry millions during that period. Now China has its own Fashion Week in Shanghai, so my client might be right in the long run.

But the lesson then was:

In planning, get second and third opinions—and listen to them.

Marketing a Service, Not a Product

The "Features" of a Service

Products have features, which in turn produce benefits. A Porsche engine's high torque, as one example, produces the thrill of the near G forces of sudden acceleration.

Services, by contrast, do not have features. Instead, they have resumes with five subcategories.

The first is *training*. This is the engineer from MIT, the cosmetologist from the Aveda Institute, and the Iowa Writers' Workshop freelance writer. It also is the architect who worked under Frank Gehry and the people of Invisible Fence, each trained in the unique security requirements for different breeds of dogs. We regard training in something as some evidence of the ability to perform it.

This also is true of the second "feature" of a service, its *achievements*. This is the law firm with a collection of Super Lawyers, the ad agency with shelves full of One Show Awards, or the travel agency named *Traveler's Magazine* Greek Travel Agency of the Year. This also is a firm's annual growth, an investment firm's annual rate of return, and Lowry Hill's remarkable record of client retention. (I once asked its then managing partner if his firm had ever lost a client. "Only to death," he answered.)

The third "feature" of a service is its *experiences*. This is Doug Nill, the former farmworker and farm writer marketing his legal services to victims of farm accidents; the avid motorcyclists who pitch the Harley-Davidson business; the therapist who lost her mother young and who specializes in grief. These experiences convey to a prospective client that this service provider has walked in that prospect's shoes; they understand.

The second category of experiences includes the architecture firm that has handled multiple sustainability projects, the twenty-one years of experience of the average Lowry Hill advisor, and the veterinarian with a decade of specialized work in canine oncology. Experiences play into our belief that considerable practice makes services closer to perfect.

A service's fourth feature is its *credentials*. In its most popular form, this is the impressive client list. Lowry Hill's list of dozens of Fortune 100 executives and Hellenic Adventures' list that includes the Academy Award–winning Greek actress, the late Olympia Dukakis.

The final feature of a service, but only of some services, is its differentiating *approach*. This was Lowry Hill's then-unique team approach to "total wealth management," combining an investment manager with a financial specialist, and this still is Greene Espel's democratic approach to its firm's management. But it is challenging to create, and all but impossible to sustain, any competitive advantage to a service approach; you cannot patent one. If your approach proves popular, others will copy it—restaurants that deliver are among the recent examples—so the first-mover advantage does not exist in service markets.

So, these are the "features" of a service: the elements of its resume. But what are the benefits of any or all of these features to a prospect?

In each case, it's assurance. Because prospects cannot be sure of the outcomes from a service, they ultimately place what feels like the safest bet. They bet on the service with the most assuring combination of training, experiences, achievements, and credentials.

That is the benefit of every feature of a service firm: comfort—the comfort that comes from the assurances that the service can and will perform.

Are your training, experiences, achievements, and other credentials enough? How might you add to them?

Services: The Positioning Fallacy

The first thing to understand about positioning in service marketing is that there are only six major positions—and chances are that none of them apply to you.

But don't worry, as you will see.

There is the Historic Leader. It's Skidmore, Owings & Merrill in architecture; BBDO, Ogilvy, and DDB in advertising; and McKinsey & Company in consulting.

There is the Innovator. Famously, it was Billy Beane in baseball; George Lois and now Wieden + Kennedy in advertising; and the audacious Frank Gehry in architecture, taking over the crown from Frank Lloyd Wright.

The next pair of related positions are the dollars and cents positions: the Premium Provider and the Discounter: Bergdorf Goodman and Walmart.

Next, we find the One-Stop Shop: everything you need under one roof. These are the national twenty most prominent law firms and the Big Four accounting firms. Its opposite is the Specialist: the intellectual property law firm, the agricultural advertising firm, the literary agent who handles only romance novels.

But as you begin to study positioning in every service market, you realize something critical. Positioning, and the branding that follows from it, only applies to large-scale services. The smaller service enterprise cannot occupy a position because, as Ries & Trout famously set forth in their landmark book, positions do not exist in the real world. Positions exist only in prospects' minds. If you are not well known, you have no position or brand.

So, Harleys are manly, and Manolo Blahniks are sexy. And in services, Wieden + Kennedy is incredibly creative, and McKinsey seems to run the planet. But a smaller service does not occupy any branded position in a prospect's mind because it is barely known, if known at all. A smaller service is nothing more in your brain than a name you might have heard.

If you are among 999 services in 1,000, you simply do not have the scale or the resources to buy a position, or a brand, in your prospects' minds. (The idea of branding a person, without having Paris Hilton's or Kim Kardashian's multimillions to buy that brand with, is even more foolish.)

But you can build one asset in their mind.

It is an absurdly powerful asset called "I have heard of you."

And you build that position with another powerful and underestimated asset: a name that imprints in people's minds, ideally instantly.

This is because service prospects ultimately choose the service that makes them feel most comfortable. (It is the one reason service clients most often give for continuing to work with a service. Over and over again, these clients say, "I just feel comfortable with them.")

And if your name seems familiar to a prospect, that person assumes there must be a good reason; you are a superior service from being familiar by name alone. And the prospect, like all human beings, draws inferences from that. "Someone must have told me about you. Maybe I read about you."

And best of all: "So you must be good."

This is what we human beings do; we infer whole sets of "facts" from a single one because we want to feel we are making intelligent choices. This results in one of our famous traits, which is to routinely conclude too much from too little. (We also tend to badly overestimate our intelligence—the famous Dunning-Kruger effect.)

But we humans need to infer. It saves us something we treasure: time, particularly in our time-squeezed age.

So this is the position you want to occupy in a prospect's mind: *I have heard of you.* This means your marketing can benefit enormously from a sticky name.

Think of people from Prince to Lady Gaga. And companies from Chipotle and Google to Spanx and Lululemon.

Instead a seizing a position, seize "I've-heard-of-you-ness."

P.S. A helpful guide to "stickiness" is Chip and Dan Heath's aptly titled bestseller, Made to Stick.

Products Sell Benefits, Services Sell Assurances

You've probably heard this famous piece of advice before, perhaps dozens of times.

You don't sell features. You sell benefits.

To illustrate this, think about buying a car. What benefits to you can a car promise?

There's the benefit of status. Mercedes and Rolls-Royce promise that.

There's the thrill of going zero to sixty before a police officer notices. Corvette and Porsche promise that benefit.

There's the comfort of knowing you can drive the car for years without ever seeing a repair man. A Toyota and Lexus provide that.

And there are the benefits of saving money with a Volkswagen, saving money on gas with a Honda Accord, or helping save our planet with a Prius.

Think of the different toothpastes and the different benefits they promise: whiter teeth, fewer cavities, tartar control, tar reduction and whitening for smokers, better breath, even better breath without having to taste regular Listerine, and the special psychological benefits of "natural" toothpastes.

People who buy products are looking for one of many different benefits. The job of product marketers is to identify all of those sought benefits and create a niche of offerings to meet them.

But now let's look at services. Does the same principle apply?

You need your tax return filed. What do you want? You want to pay as little as possible—that one benefit, always.

You want to invest with a financial planner and you want the highest possible return on your investment, balanced against the risk you are willing to take. That one benefit, always.

You are struggling with anxiety. You want relief. That one benefit, only.

Every day has become a bad hair day. What do you want? A flattering haircut. That one benefit, always.

Within any market category, why would anyone offer different benefits when everyone wants the same one thing: an answer to one specific need?

So, does it make sense to think about benefits in marketing a service? Only in realizing that you always are selling this one benefit, always: *the assurance you can perform the task.*

The benefit that every service sells, in every category, is assurance—the assurance of knowing you can deliver on the promise—which, again, is all a service is at the time you sell it: a promise that at some future date, you will perform a certain task and achieve the outcome.

You don't sell benefits. You sell assurance—the one thing that overcomes the feelings every prospect has: fear, uncertainty, and doubt.

Don't sell us. Assure us.

The Masters of Assurance

It all started with a bad road trip.

Disgusted by the dingy motels he encountered on a 1952 trip to Washington, DC, from his hometown of Memphis, Tennessee, Kemmons Wilson decided to build a chain of motels with the exact same rooms everywhere, each of them air-conditioned, carpeted wall-to-wall, and offering a telephone by each bed. And that August, Wilson opened his first motel in his hometown, which he named after the famous Christmas movie of that day: *Holiday Inn.*

Five hundred fifty miles away, in Des Plaines, Illinois, Ray Kroc had decided this approach would work with hamburgers, too. And the burger business needed something. Hamburger "joints" in 1950s America were just that—noisy hangouts with rancid-smelling restrooms and bubble gum–chomping waitresses. The spread of "carhop drive-ins" succeeded at drawing leather jacket–wearing boys to ogle the female carhops but repelled parents of young children, who didn't want to expose them to the older kids' mating rituals.

Seeing the appeal of a Holiday Inn of hamburger restaurants, and the potential for a hamburger restaurant that could draw these parents and their younger children, Kroc persuaded Richard and Maurice McDonald, the owners of several successful hamburger spots in California and one in Phoenix, Arizona, to make him their national franchise manager.

Within years, Holiday Inns had three hundred thousand beds and Ray Kroc's McDonald's was becoming the phenomenon that today earns more money than anyone can comprehend: half-a-million dollars a minute.

McDonald's did not become a phenomenon, however, by coming up with the fast-food concept first. White Castle already was thirty-four years old, and the Insta-Burger King started a year before Kroc opened his first McDonald's, in Illinois. Kroc's genius, instead, was in seeing the value of utter consistency—in quality, taste, speed, and cleanliness—everywhere a traveler would go. That consistency—even consistent "merely good-enoughness"—would give parents confidence of getting the exact same quality, every day and everywhere.

Wilson and Kroc knew that service prospects fear bad experiences far more than they covet great ones, and that what we want most is to be assured of a good-enough experience. These two men realized we might not love McDonald's burgers or Holiday Inn's cookie-cutter rooms, but would love always getting just what we expected.

The great services know it: what we want most from a service is a result we can count on.

Prudential assures us we can count on them: they're the Rock of Gibraltar.

Allstate assures us we're in good hands with them.

UPS assures us they will deliver because they run the tightest ship in the shipping business.

FedEx assures that our package absolutely, positively will get there overnight.

And for years, Sears Auto Centers captured it perfectly, while playing on our pervasive doubts about the integrity of auto repair centers: "We install confidence."

Except when we are dealing with masters of uniformity like McDonald's and Holiday Inn, we never know just what we might get from a service until we actually get it. This means that what every service must sell, first—this for the last time, I promise—is assurance. You must convince us you can and will deliver.

As Kemmons Wilson and Ray Kroc discovered, to the delight of their heirs, the more absolutely and positively we believe you can deliver, the more likely we are to choose you.

How can you assure prospects you can deliver?

The Force of Focus

Little by little, one travels far.
—J. R. R. Tolkien

Taco Bell started as a hot dog stand in San Bernardino, California.

Gap was a record store in San Francisco.

Nordstrom was a tiny shoe store in Seattle.

And Marriott was an A&W root beer stand in Washington, DC.

Both Mr. Wells and Mr. Fargo started American Express and Wells Fargo, respectively, as express mail services, the first in Buffalo, New York, the second in San Francisco.

3M once made only sandpaper, John Deere only plows, and Lamborghini only tractors.

Disney was a black-and-white cartoon production company—the mouse originally was called Mortimer—for almost twenty-five years. Princeton was a training school for ministers. Amazon sold only books, which today account for only 7 percent of the company's sales.

No great business tried to be many things to many people; each focused on being one good thing.

Each found something they did well, earned a reputation for it, and launched.

Most entrepreneurs resist this advice, for fear that focusing on a single market will reduce their appeal. They try to be jacks-of-all-trades, which appeal to no one.

Skadden, Arps started as a law firm specializing in mergers and acquisitions. Clients with other legal problems decided that attorneys who could master the complexities of mergers and acquisitions could handle almost anything.

Today, Skadden does just that. With twenty-three offices and over five hundred employees, it's the largest law firm in America.

McKinsey & Company started by showing clients how to apply accounting principles. Clients were impressed and asked for more. Today, the firm has over 105 offices and over 17,000 employees and consults on more areas of business than can fit on this page.

Every great enterprise started in a tiny niche.

You must, too.

Focus. Getting bigger starts by thinking smaller.

Focus, Focus, Focus

The Old Economy was built around big companies that offered a full range of services. Marketers pushed "one-stop shopping" as a powerful and popular selling message. It was good to be the Department Store.

But both for products and services, department stores continue to disappear—there are only four mega-agencies in advertising today—while the boutiques thrive.

These boutiques are attacking the markets.

But we find we must specialize in this age of growing complexity. No one can credibly claim expertise in both federal tax and partnerships and corporations, for example. The remarkable explosion of financial options means no one can be an expert on each option, as evidenced by my conversation with the top executive of a large variable annuity company.

I asked, "Can you really keep up on all the options just in variable annuities?"

He looked down and shrugged. "No one can."

Realizing this, we actively seek out specialists.

And then there's the massively competitive business created by outsourcing and downsizing. Thus was born Freelance Nation. Overnight, employees became Businesses of One, each now having to sell their services to one company and then the next. As of today, America is a nation of fifty-three million freelancers—one worker in every three.

And they are flooding the market, including yours. They are financial advisors, executive coaches, cosmetic dentists, personal trainers, and therapists. In 1985, there were 653,668 lawyers in America, not many years after the Chief Justice of the United State had warned of "a glut of lawyers." Our glut now runneth over; we have over 1,300,000 active attorneys today. In 1971, American universities awarded 21,000 bachelor's and 1,050 master's degrees in accounting. This year's comparable numbers will exceed 61,500 and 22,000, respectively—a nearly fourfold increase in the number of newly minted accountants in less than five decades.

In what's been dubbed "the Gig Economy," some actually wear several hats and carry more than one business card. You can find them in almost every Starbucks, and new ones every week.

This is a key cause of hypercompetition and a key influence on your effective marketing communications strategies. It's now a five-thousand-horse race.

You cannot win by entering the big race; focus on a smaller one first.

Focus & Your Sheer Uniqueness

I was, briefly, stunned.

One of my first clients was an eleven-person accounting firm.

During our first meeting, I asked the key marketing question, "What makes you different? We need to get your message focused."

The managing partner shrugged. "Nothing really. Accountants are accountants."

I was jolted for a second but kept moving. "I'm sure you are different," I said. "No two groups of people behave the same. I'm sure we can find your distinction."

"Honestly," the stern-looking fellow said. "We're the same. Just pretty good accountants."

I looked at him without responding for several seconds, hoping he might come to his senses; you can go years, after all, without hearing from one man who thinks he is merely pretty good. But I was hearing that from ten of them.

Fortunately, a story came to me, and I knew instantly it was perfect, because we were in Minneapolis. It's the story of flour.

For over 750 years, wheat flour had been just flour, the product of grinding wheat seeds into a powder. In movies about the Old West, you often see scenes of a woman going into "the General Store" for some flour, sold from a large barrel just marked "Flour." Flour was flour.

And then Cadwallader C. Washburn came along and, in 1866, founded a flour mill on the banks of the Mississippi. By 1880, he decided to take samples of his best flours to Cincinnati to enter the medal competitions in the first International Miller's Exhibition. And Washburn boarded the train back to Minneapolis carrying all three medals.

The medals gave him an inspiration: let's brand our flour.

And within years, in the eyes of housewives everywhere, flour no longer was just flour: *Gold Medal* flour was better.

This phenomenon—turning identical commodities into distinctive branded products that could be sold at a premium—happened everywhere in America. In Pittsburgh, H. J. Heinz decided he could brand and market another commodity sold in those General Store tubs: pickles. In Crockett, California, two fellows decided that Americans would pay more for "pure cane sugar from Hawaii," and C&H Sugar was born, and soon booming. Years later, in Maryland, Frank Perdue, ignoring dozens of friends who insisted he had gone batty, decided he could brand chickens. ("With what, Frank," he must have heard, "the Circle S Ranch on their little chicken butts?")

The last laugh, of course, was Frank's; Perdue Chicken is now a $6 billion business.

After telling these stories, I suggested to the accountants that if people can distinguish flour, pickles, sugar, and chickens, you can distinguish a group of accountants. No two people are the same, after all. Two groups of different people are even less similar.

I told them to try this test.

You've seen hundreds of actors in your life. Not only are no two actors the same; *no two are very much alike.* Leonardo DiCaprio is nothing like Tom Hanks, who is nothing like Johnny Depp, Morgan Freeman, or Matthew McConaughey. And who on earth is like Joaquin Phoenix?

Yes, some movie buffs compare George Clooney to Cary Grant, but the comparison ends after dark, handsome, and self-deprecating. (It turns out, by the way, that even Cary Grant wasn't Cary Grant. A reporter once asked him what it was like to learn that so many men wanted to be Cary Grant. He answered, "I don't blame them. Hell, *I'd* like to be Cary Grant.")

I could tell two were movie fans; both men's eyebrows were raised and they were nodding.

"You are human beings," I said. "Being different is inherent in being human. The question is not *whether* you are different; it's *how* you are different, and how we can convey that to draw more clients to you."

We tell our children they are special. We aren't making that up; each of us is unique. Marketing's job is to convey that uniqueness.

So tell us: What makes you, you?

Selling Assurance: Goodbye, USP

From the 1940s forward, marketing thinking was dominated by the Unique Selling Proposition, a term concocted by ad man Rosser Reeves to describe successful ad campaigns for products.

But every service is unique because every person is, and no two collections of people behave identically.

And when someone needs a service, no one cares if it's unique. What they care about is, does it perform?

The often-used substitute for the USP, the Value Proposition, doesn't work well for services, either. Proposing that you offer some value does not sound compelling. And by the very act of going into business, every service proposes that it can bring some unique value to those it serves.

Services need a different tool—something other than the USP or Value Proposition—because services differ from products in yet another way. A product needs little proof, as the familiar expression reminds us: *The proof is in the pudding.* The performance car leaps when you hit the accelerator, the rich, hoppy IPA beer tastes rich and hoppy, and the high-resolution screen looks lifelike. The Product Proposition—performance, rich and hoppy, and lifelike—is enough; the proof comes immediately in your experience—or it doesn't, and the product disappears. And you can test a product beforehand or try a sample, to see if it meets its promise. If it overpromised, it dies and takes the brand, which made that false promise, with it.

In other words, a product proves itself.

But services go through a different screen from their prospective buyers. For example, how do you know if a consultant can help you? That the remodeler can finish before Christmas? That the cab will arrive on time? There's no test drive, sample sip, or visit to Best Buy to assure you.

There's no pudding in a service, so there's no proof.

For a service, then, a mere *proposition* isn't enough. Your prospect—again, riddled with fear, uncertainty, and doubt—needs reassurance. She needs *evidence*.

What evidence shows you will perform?

A Key: Your Key Evidence Statement

In marketing a service, talk is cheap; what you say doesn't matter. It's what you can prove.

That's why we all need Key Evidence Statements. And they're easy to create.

First, identify your Target. Perhaps it's small (ten to fifty employees) business owners, a couple with at least $500,000 in investible assets, or gay men and women dealing with a major life loss, for example. But write down your Target.

Now, your Claim: How can your services make the lives of people in that Target better?

And finally, list the evidence that shows, or at least suggests, that you can deliver on that promise. This becomes your Key Evidence Statement.

To see this in action, let's go to the wealth managers of Lowry Hill, at their relaunch.

The LH Target: couples with at least $10 million in investible assets,

The LH Claim: We can manage *every* aspect of a client's financial life, including investing, estate planning, establishing charitable foundations—everything a busy and affluent couple needs under a single roof while achieving maximum *real* return on investments—or true return after fees and taxes.

Now, what was the evidence that Lowry Hill could deliver on that promise—specifically, what were their accomplishments and credentials? (And lead with accomplishments; credentials only hint at what you might be able to accomplish.) And did they employ any process that increased the likelihood of delivering on that Claim? So here were their accomplishments:

Passionate client testimonials.

A five- and ten-year record of investment performance that beat both the Dow and Standard & Poor's indexes.

Their bandwagon client list: thirty-three CEOs and clients in forty-four states and seventy-four countries with an aggregate of over $6 billion in investible assets with the firm.

A client retention rate of almost 100 percent.

Eleven percent annual growth.

And here was their process:

A 5:1 Lowry partner-to-client ratio, which made possible lavish focus on the client. Rather than assign just an investment advisor to each client, Lowry Hill assigned a two-person team: a senior investment partner and a senior financial partner trained in all aspects of personal finance.

Finally, their credentials:

MBAs, Masters in Finance, JD degrees, published authors.

"Wow."

This was compelling evidence that Lowry Hill could deliver on their Claim—and had done so repeatedly.

And they continued. Over the next decade, the firm *sextupled* their assets under management.

This is the Golden Swan case, to be sure. But this sets up the ideal process:

Identify your Target, Claim, and Evidence.

Sometimes, Your Evidence Comes First

Decades ago, when I launched Beckwith Partners, what was my Key Evidence—my accomplishments and credentials?

Former award-winning creative supervisor and copywriter of a national and international award-winning ad agency.

Winner of the American Marketing Association's Effie for the year's most effective business-to-business campaign (educational computer systems) and local Effie for most effective business-to-business campaign (physiologic pacemaker systems and support).

Former law clerk to a federal judge.

Six years of legal practice.

Honors graduate of Stanford University.

Well, it's not hard for you to see what I should have chosen as my Target—law firms—and I did.

But something slowly happened that encouraged me to focus on a single Target. The Target eventually grew by itself.

Working for law firms attracted services for law firms: deposition summary providers and jury research firms. Even better, my work for law firms led executives in other professional services—particularly accounting firms—to decide I could help them, too. And working for affluent clients like lawyers convinced professional services that targeted the affluent—notably, wealth management firms—to decide I might be able to help them, too.

So law begat accounting, financial services, and eventually larger consulting firms, particularly firms that sell well-educated wisdom and intelligence to sophisticated, well-educated clients.

And this worked perfectly, for another reason of significance: I learned I did not want to work with lawyers.

I didn't enjoy practicing law. I hate rules and don't like compromising, two career-killing traits in that line of work. And with at least two remarkable exceptions—my four most beloved clients include an attorney and two recovering attorneys—lawyers are notoriously awful clients. They are certain, among their other endearing traits, that, if they had the time, they can do your job better than you.

You might find yourself and your business in a similar position. You look at the Target for which your evidence is most compelling but decide you don't want to spend your years serving that Target. It's not your passion. And that's a wonderful reason not to do any task for very long.

But don't worry. Serve that Target well enough and, just as mine did, your Target will grow itself, diversifying into profitable areas that truly interest you.

Good work will make your Target bigger; great work will make it so big you can hit it blindfolded.

What Target will find your Evidence most appealing?

What Do I Do with the Key Evidence Statement?

Repeat it, *everywhere.*

Get it "above the fold" in your website, weave it into your email sign-off, lead with it in your first meeting with your prospect.

And then look at it and ask: What might I do to make it more powerful? Should I submit an article on my specialty to a publication that reaches my Target? (That's ideal, as millions can tell you.)

What recognition in your work should you work toward? What Super lists, local publications' "Best" lists, speeches at nearby colleges, or other activities will make many of your prospects decide you must be pretty good? Set a goal for this year of adding at least one piece of evidence to your Key Evidence list.

Work your Evidence, and work on adding to it.

The Farm Boy Hits the Bull's-Eye

Too many years ago, my friend Doug Nill came bursting into my office. He'd had a Eureka! moment.

Doug was a young family law lawyer, mentioned elsewhere in this book. We had worked together to substantially build up his divorce law practice.

And, like me, he didn't find that very much fun. Divorce law simply isn't.

But he had a brainstorm. Doug came from a farming family in North Dakota and still worked the fall harvest. Farming stayed long enough in his blood that when he headed off to North Dakota State for college, he majored in Agricultural Economics, then became the editor of a five-state publication, *Farm & Ranch Guide*, while fitting in graduating from law school and winning a coveted legal clerkship with a federal judge in Iowa.

We were a natural fit, as this book will explore later: two kids from farming areas, former clerks to federal judges, with a shared ambivalence for the practice of law—mine for law of any kind, Doug for the unending and too-sad trauma of divorce law.

But Doug had decided on a path other than mine. He knew farms and farming, and that many parts of the Dakotas were not served by lawyers with other than very general practices. They handled whatever case came over their phone line. And Doug had the law clerk credentials, several years of trial practice, and an idea.

"What if we do small space ads in farmer publications, targeting farm accidents? The damages can be overwhelming—a complete loss of the ability to work the farm, most obviously. And the accidents happen all the time."

"Don't I know," I said. "My dad was a doctor surrounded by Holstein dairy farmers. Can't count how many hands he treated after they went through hay balers."

"That's right, Harry. And farmers don't trust lawyers, but they will trust one of their own—a kid who still works the harvest for his family farm. We have what you've called 'alikeness.'"

Essentially, Doug was looking at his evidence—in this case, his background, which might have seemed irrelevant to the practice of law—and deciding on his Target.

I didn't need convincing; he'd nailed it. We immediately went to work and ran a small ad, which ran in *Dakota Farmer*, that stressed that Doug was a farm kid with an agriculture degree and a successful big-city trial practice.

Flash-forward to 2002. The Minnesota Supreme Court reaffirmed a decision awarding Doug's clients $52 million. And then to 2006, when Doug was named Minnesota Attorney of the Year. And then to 2008, when a St. Paul judge awarded Doug's class action farmer/clients $62 million.

A truly nice guy, Doug now sponsors our local Run, Walk, and Roll Against Bullying and does weeks of pro bono work every year. But his main accomplishment is that he finished first, and got first to that finish by seeing exactly where to start: he saw a trait that might appeal to a Target, fired at the Target, and won his profession's equivalent of the lottery.

Look at your background. What group of prospects might respond well to it?

Maybe your Target is, in a sense, you.

The New USP for Services: The EBC

Doug Nill promised farmers he could help them recover damages for accidents, and backed it with evidence that he knew farmers, had studied and written about farming, and had proven himself in a successful Minneapolis trial practice.

That was his EBC, or Evidence-Backed Claim, and it changed his life.
What is your Evidence-Backed Claim?

The EBC in Practice

A friend's in-law approached me for help marketing her psychology counseling services.

I probed and discovered that she understood grief all too well. At sixteen, she lost her mother to cancer and had suffered another great loss in her twenties.

Before opening her own office, she had spent years triaging dozens of calls a day from people suffering from depression for a major health care company. People suffering from depression. She empathized. Their voices could have been hers.

And she helped them.

So how should she market herself? She began by stressing the need to specialize. I was certain her focus should be on what she knew best: loss. She had been there and heard and felt it for decades, and passionately wanted no one to suffer what she had.

Her EBC? "For eleven years, I have helped over ten thousand people suffering a great loss and have suffered two personally. I have helped them and myself and am certain I can help you."

Might this be stronger? Yes. And it will be, as she gains more experience. But this illustrates what every service needs: an Evidence-Backed Claim.

Begin by creating an EBC.

Focusing: Name It, Frame It, Claim It

I have a simple way to describe the simplest positioning process for every service:

Name it, frame it, and claim it.

The first task is to name it, of course. In a world of hypercompetition and limited brain space, having a short and memorable name can be indispensable.

The second step—describing the service—is not as easy as it may seem, and is critical, too.

Then, the claim. What makes you distinctive—not utterly unique, perhaps, but distinctive?

To illustrate it, I will follow my regular advice to you by telling you a story—four, actually.

NFC One: The Bold Litigators

The law firm Greene Espel started in my living room in 1990. They were star attorneys—two senior partners and two rising stars—from a much larger law firm.

They were committed to specializing only in litigation. They also were committed to doing only what they were certain they could do best. Our first ad conveyed this clearly: "We will take your case if we are ideally suited to it. If we are not, we will find the best law firm for you."

The message worked. For months, lawyers would stop one of the four Greene Espel attorneys and say, "You're the guys who will refer prospects to competitors—wow."

It was a compelling promise: Greene Espel were offering to provide the best litigation team for a client, even if that team was playing in another stadium.

The firm flew. Today, six times larger, they have been recognized by several publications as one of America's best litigation boutiques.

We're the specialists, or we'll find you one.

NFC Two: The Dog People

You probably think of Invisible Fence as a fence company. But it actually is a nationwide network of franchised dealers trained in dog behavior, right down to the distinctive behaviors of different breeds. (A beagle always finds its way home, for example, so you only need a fence if there are predators in your neighborhood and a physical structure is required to keep them out.) Not surprisingly, these owners were drawn to the business because they love dogs—something every dog owner understands and appreciates.

So it's not just a fence. It's an expert service.

And IF's emphasis was not on fencing. It was on the total package of services and products to ensure every dog's safety. These folks knew dogs, breed by breed.

Only an expert on your breed of dog can protect your breed of dog.

The Greek Wizard's NFC

Hellenic Adventures: Greek Travel Specialists

This was easy. Hear the name of its president and chief tour guide—Leftheris Papageorgiou—and you know you are getting a Greek travel expert. Even famous Greeks, notably the Academy Award–winning actress Olympia Dukakis, have chosen Leftheris to lead their tours.

With six syllables, this name was at last two syllables too long, but I underestimated the importance of names then. And it was better to spend their limited resources on handsome and lovingly written direct mail pieces that would bring in more clients.

Those mailers ended up working well enough, and their name had been around long enough that we decided the name was not handicapping them.

Travel + Leisure has named this one of the world's three best Greek travel services, and the *Los Angeles Times* has named its tour among its "Top Ten Tours for Thinking People."

This may illustrate the power of sheer passion. I've never worked with anyone more passionate about his work—his beloved country—and more fun to work with. They say, "You never can go home again," but this man is a passionate exception.

Only a Greek can show you the real Greece.

The Caring Providers' NFC

Primrose: Living with Memory Loss

I think this Santa Rosa, California, enterprise was called Heritage Landing, or some similar name that scratched across my blackboard, when they approached me through the Silicon Valley venture capital firm Institutional Venture Partners.

I immediately saw that these people were taking a fresh and informed approach. Experts call Alzheimer's "the wandering disease." Its sufferers like to walk to relieve their stress but are too apt to walk out a door and disappear. Primrose decided to deal with this.

They built beautiful walking paths lined with gardens, along with playgrounds for visiting grandchildren, to encourage entire families to visit the patient.

We chose the name Primrose to focus the message on the outside, not the inside. The insides of these facilities always have challenged people and their visitors, after all, because people who have memory loss suffer from incontinence, too. So it's not easy to keep these places smelling lovely and feeling "prim and proper." Plus, the name "Primrose" was not in common use—it satisfied the need for an unusual name. Finally, you may have heard the expression "the primrose path." Primrose featured flower-lined paths. So this was perfect.

To further stress "outside," we crafted their logo from a flower. (As one of only five logos I both designed and illustrated, this one holds a special place for me.)

The flower also appears to be both a cross, suggesting faith and hope, and a person opening her arms to the visitor, promising "You are loved here."

The theme also stresses "living" in the fullest sense, something the patients' loved ones dearly want in dealing with what is known, accurately and sadly, as "the long goodbye."

Other facilities looked and felt liked institutions. Primrose, by immediate contrast, was special.

Your loved one needs a home, not a hospital.

Pricing

Money Talks: So What Does Your Price Say?

Welcome to another strange but true story—told to me not once, but twice, at the annual meeting of one of America's premier consulting firms.

The story begins on a sunny September afternoon in Franklin Lakes, New Jersey. David, an experienced consultant, calls on a Fortune 500 prospect. The prospect is impressed but balks at the consultant's $2,750-per-day fee.

They part.

Three weeks later, David takes a job in the New York office of a well-known national consulting firm. Two days later, he runs into the prospect at a hot dog stand inside Yankee Stadium.

"I'm with Juggernaut now," he tells her.

A week later, she retains David for consulting—at his new fee of $3,500 per day.

Flash-forward to a speech in Denver, Colorado, two months later. After the address, I notice a man beelining toward me from the back row. When he arrives at the front of the stage, he's nearly breathless.

He tells me the story of Charles. Shopping in the Cherry Creek neighborhood of Denver, he spotted the Ralph Lauren frames he wanted at $115. He left and drove to a second store six minutes away, where he spotted the same frames priced at just $70.

"Are these the tortoiseshell Ralph Laurens?" Charles asked. The young male clerk said they were.

"Why are they only $70?"

"That's just what our owner decided."

"Are you sure they are the Ralph Laurens?"

Hard to say no to that question when Mr. Lauren's name is emblazoned on the glasses, but Charles felt uncertain and left. Two days later, he returned, saw that the frames still were priced at $70, and again questioned the price.

Three days later, Charles returned to the store for the third time. The day before, the clerk had told the owner to mark up the frames to $115.

Charles said, "I'll take them."

There's more.

Outside the auditorium after a speech in Toronto less than a year later, I was approached by a man whose comment left me anxious. "I need a word with you."

I immediately worried that my speech had offended him.

He returned from the restroom. "My wife is an interior decorator here in the province," he began. "Before she read your book, she was charging the going rate here, which was $55 per hour."

"That sounds attractive," I said.

"Yes, but she wasn't that busy. She was billing fewer than twenty hours a week."

I flinched, certain that a boom was about to fall.

"Then she read your book and decided to start charging $120 an hour. And you know what happened?"

Chapter 7? I thought.

"Her business picked up so much that now I have to do all the housework."

These stories demonstrate the remarkable influence of price on your prospects' decisions. Price becomes a proxy for quality; a higher price suggests that even though the prospect cannot inspect your service and see its quality, the quality must be there. The higher the price, the higher the presumed quality.

What does your price say about you?

Two Reminders on Price

Threatened with death by the arrival of cheaper Japanese guitars in this country, Gibson guitar executives came up with a crazy solution over drinks in a Nashville bar one night. "Let's just raise the prices, take the money, and run." So they raised their prices.

Naturally, and overnight, this increased their margins on every guitar they sold. But something else happened, quite remarkably: they sold even more guitars at the higher price.

Your price is not just your price. It is a quality cue.

We think "price resistance" means only our resistance to high prices. But we resist low prices, too, and are tempted by higher ones. When Uma Thurman marvels over her famous five-dollar shake in the movie *Pulp Fiction*, as a favorite example, John Travolta cannot resist.

"What, does it have bourbon in it or something?" And finally, of course, he has to ask: "You think I could have a sip of that?"

A high price sends a quality cue.

If they come for your low price, they will leave for a lower one.

Two Favorite Pricing Lessons

A visiting American woman was strolling along a street in Paris when she spotted Picasso sketching at a sidewalk café. She approached him, then made a bold request.

"Could you just do a quick sketch of me? I'd naturally pay you."

The busy artist obliged. In just minutes, there she was: in an original Picasso.

With her right hand shaking as she held the sketch, she asked, "And what do I owe you?"

"Two thousand francs," he said.

Startled yet still grateful, the woman felt compelled to challenge him.

"But it only took you three minutes," she implored.

"No," Picasso said. "It took me all my life."

A carpenter was invited to a woman's home to solve a nagging problem. Try as she might, nothing she had attempted had fixed her squeaky floor.

The carpenter arrived, took several quick steps above and near the squeak, then pulled three nails from his bag. He pounded the nails into the floor, then stood up and walked over the spot. The squeak was gone. It had taken him just minutes.

He wrote out a bill and handed it to the delighted homeowner. It read:

"Pounding: $5.

"Knowing where to pound: $70."

Charge by the years, not the hour.

Two More Important Dispatches

Timberland was under siege from the makers of higher-priced Sperry Topsiders, the classic boat shoe. They increased advertising and pegged the standard retail price for their shoes 20 percent higher than Sperry.

Sales leapt.

In his excellent book *Influence*, Robert Cialdini tells the story of a Native American store in Santa Fe, New Mexico, which suffered from an oversupply of turquoise jewelry. (As you may have experienced, there is so much turquoise jewelry in Santa Fe that the insides of many stores look like the bottom of swimming pools.)

Before leaving on vacation, the owner instructed her assistant to cut the prices on all the pieces by half. When the owner returned from the vacation, she got the thrilling news: the jewelry had all been sold. Proof that discounting pays?

Not at all.

Her assistant had misread her note and *doubled* all the prices.

Your price is not just your price. It is a clue. It communicates what you and the market believe is the value of your service. If your price is high, you're very good. If it's very low, you're inexpensive. If you are priced in the middle, you are in the middle.

However you price yourself, realize your price sends a message. Price talks. In today's too busy and overcommunicated world, prospects look for tiny clues, and few say more than what your price says about you.

What does your price say?

Premium Pricing and Passionate Fans

So, a higher price sends a strong quality signal, which may be reason enough for you to considering nudging your fees or prices upward.

But there are two more, it appears.

Researchers tested premium pricing with organic coffee. For pur-
poses of explaining the test, the market price per pound was $10.00.
The subjects for the test said they would be willing to pay a $2 premium
for free-trade coffee.

But what if you charged them $18 instead—for the exact same cof-
fee? How would those customers react?

With a passion, it turned out. The $18 buyers were far more pas-
sionate advocates than the $12 and $10 buyers.

And these advocates became fans in a deeper way. Just like many
sports fans, who can recite the entire starting lineup of their alma
maters and the pertinent statistics of the players on their beloved team,
the $18 buyers became not just passionate users, but passionate stu-
dents of the product. They could recite almost twice as many details
about the coffee as those who tried the lower-priced coffees.

The premium buyers could not only give you the reason to buy the
product. They also could give you more reasons why you should, which
would make them even more effective as word-of-mouth salespeople.

*To increase satisfaction, increasing your prices may be a good
place to start.*

The Mess in the Middle

Selling the Invisible warned readers of a growing trend. I called it "The
Deadly Middle." Eight years and days after the book appeared, Sharon
Stone made this phenomenon famous.

Invited to present the Best Actress award at the Academy Awards,
Ms. Stone went to her ample closet just the evening before and picked
out her five favorite pieces. Following her friend Ellen DeGeneres's suggestion, Stone finally chose three: a Valentino skirt, an Armani dress

that she would wear as a coat, and a black Gap T-shirt. The message was Expensive, Extravagant, and Could Not Be Cheaper.

Stone was doing what Americans everywhere were doing: trading up or trading down. We were buying either the most expensive items, or the least expensive ones. Items that didn't offer one or the other—the best quality or best price—were suffering

They still are. They are caught in the Deadly Middle.

What might explain this?

Think of the feeling of owning something special and uncommon. It activates your sense of self.

Knowing you have purchased a special item also makes you feel wise. It's why expensive clothing is called "investment clothing."

Similarly, the least expensive item appeals to the side of your ego that praises you for spending wisely. It salutes you for not spending $40 for a black T-shirt when a $9 Gap tee looks just as flattering—and leaves you with $30 more to spend on something else.

But what about the item that is neither exceptionally good—and recognized by others—nor one that saves you the most? What satisfaction does it give you? Very little. Choosing those products makes us uncomfortable, because they offer us too little satisfaction for our investment.

That's the problem with a merely good service for a good price. It's not great at anything. And it doesn't make us feel good about ourselves.

It's caught in the Deadly Middle.

Watch out for the Deadly Middle.

Lowest Price Costs You Twice

You pay twice when you charge very little.

You pay in lost revenue. You make less money.

But you pay a second time, and too many people fail to realize this. You pay in reputation—you earn less regard.

When you're priced the lowest, you are the one that pays most.

Can you really afford to be the low-cost provider?

The Perils of the Low-Cost Position

Not everyone loved *Selling the Invisible*. Even though the book was a bestseller, a *Wall Street Journal* reviewer dubbed me "a jingle writer from the Midwest." (A better description of me, "a lawyer from the West Coast," might have made me sound more credible.) Citing Southwest Airlines and Walmart as proof, the reviewer insisted that I was naive in suggesting that the low-cost position in a market "kills."

It never occurred to him that mere exceptions prove rules. Of course, there was one surviving discount airline and one surviving discount retailer: just one. The implied death rate from that alone can be found in the string of bankruptcy filings in federal court: Caldor, Bradlees, Janeway, Ames, Filene's, Gordmans, National Stores, and then Sears and JC Penney—their demises were predicted in *Selling the Invisible*. And, no doubt, there will be more discount stores shutting their doors after this book goes to press.

The fact is, the low-cost position kills.

It suffers from what seems a self-evident problem: if your promise is the lowest cost, there is only room for one in your niche. Someone finds a way to offer what you offer for less, and you no longer occupy that position.

Complicating your challenge, as you try to reposition your offering, you now need to attract clients who think of your offering as cheap.

The low-cost position kills.

But What About Free?

Free isn't a price. It's a special offer with a string attached.

Amazon's free shipping isn't really free. You have to order at least $25 in merchandise. The "free" also encourages many shoppers to buy an extra item that gets their bill over $25.

"Kids eat free on Mondays" is a tactic. It charges you nothing for your little eaters and makes up for it with what it charges you and your partner.

Free often works but does nothing to disprove the idea that low pricing strategies are lethal. Because free isn't a price. It's a ploy.

Free often works. Cheapest—for a service—rarely does.

Then Why Do People Discount?

My wife, Susan, inadvertently explained this to me years ago, when she introduced me to the idea of "A High Need to Be Liked." Some people suffer from this.

They long to be liked. So they charge very little for their service because they imagine the recipient saying, "I love her. She charged me almost nothing."

Do good salespeople do this? *Never.* One of the signal traits of the best salespeople is that they never lead with price. They end with it. By the time you get to discuss the price, you are not merely willing to buy. You are eager. You've been sold. You want what they have.

If you really want to be liked, offer something so valuable people will pay more for it.

Then charge them a tiny bit less.

The Rules of Planning

To Learn, Plan

Take this comfort: no plan truly fails. Every plan teaches: learning goes in and learning comes out.

There is every chance that you will alter the plan, perhaps significantly, as events unfold. That doesn't dilute what may be the greatest value of planning: the learning that both goes into it and comes out of it.

If you want to learn how to succeed, plan.

Mistrust "Best Practices"

There's a simple way to determine the best practice for any business: ask your clients.

Mistrust anything else labeled as a best practice. What might be badass for some is simply bad for others.

Your clients know best.

See What Others Don't

The small steps in every category of business are taken by the people who discover a slightly faster way to run the same path.

These small steppers ask, "How might we do that a little better?"

The leapers ask, "Why are people doing that at all?"

If you want to take a very big step, ask, "What's the blind spot in this business? What's the one practice that everyone follows because everyone follows it—but that no one should?"

Find the blind spot.

Beware of the Loudest Voice in the Room

Plans typically fail because the group finally surrenders to its loudest and most insistent member. Unless you commit to ignoring that person's force, your plan already has been made, and you are merely a spectator to its rubber-stamping.

Ignore the noise.

Beware of the Egos

Groups are gatherings of egos, and many of the people assigned to planning suffer from strong ones. This hurts the process, so be alert to it.

Narcissists—and most planning groups endure at least one—pose a special danger. As an Oracle employee said of its CEO Larry Ellison: "What's the difference between God and Larry? God does not believe he is Larry."

Not only do narcissists feel certain they have better ideas, but their lack of empathy leads them to offend people who disagree with them.
Ignore the know-it-all.

Mistrust the Confident

Just because someone observed it doesn't mean it's true. (A corollary from law: eyewitnesses constantly get the facts wrong.)

We all overestimate what we believe we know, observed, and experienced. We are famous for our overconfidence—psychologists dub it "the Overconfidence Bias"—which also hampers successful planning.

Mistrust your knowledge—and everyone else's.

Mistrust the Past

You tried something before and saw it fail. You tried something similar at a different time.

No two events are identical. A similar event at a different time will not necessarily produce the same result.

"We tried that before" is not a reason not to try something similar now.

Mistrust Certainty (Including Your Own)

Don't seek certainty; nothing is certain. If you are waiting to be certain, you're not in the business of working. You're in the business of waiting.

It's good advice to mistrust others' confidence, and equally wise to mistrust their certainty. As Voltaire put it, "Doubt is not a pleasant condition, but certainty is absurd."

Resist Perfection

Perfect isn't the step beyond greatness. It's the barrier to it.

View Research Warily

We always hear "the research shows." But research insisted that Americans would hate *60 Minutes* and camera phones and love New Coke, PalmPilots, and the Segway.

Research never shows; it only suggests.

Go Little, Then Big

Bullets first, then cannonballs." That's management consultant and author Jim Collins's lovely metaphor for what all great companies fire. They try several approaches and then concentrate all their resources on the one that worked. You should, too.

Go little, then big.

Just Do It

In 1989, Peter Dunn and Albert Wood, scientists at Pfizer Laboratories in Sandwich, England, made an epic discovery. They believed they had found a treatment for angina, the acute chest pains and resulting struggles to breathe caused by too little blood reaching the heart. Their discovery, sildenafil citrate, promised to open the arteries of the heart and promote the needed blood flow.

In 1989, Pfizer began testing their discovery. And got two surprises.

Sildenafil citrate actually failed. The test subjects' chests still ached. But several male subjects asked if they could keep those little pills anyway.

These men's reasons sounded suspiciously flimsy to the researchers, and the men's real reasons soon became clear. As the euphemism in today's television commercials puts it, sildenafil citrate was helping make sure these men "were ready when the time was right."

Thus was born Viagra, a happy accident.

Happy accidents—the elegant synonym is serendipity—figure in a million successes. Art Fry was searching in a 3M lab for the next super-adhesive, for example, when he discovered an adhesive that barely stuck to anything. And thus were born Post-it Notes.

The discoveries of dynamite, Teflon, nylon, X-rays, photography, Rogaine, vulcanized rubber, Velcro, and anesthesia all were happy accidents. So was *Graceland*, the album that resurrected singer Paul Simon's career, and the use of feedback in rock music. (The Beatles stumbled upon it during their recording of "I Feel Fine".) The art movements known as Dada and Fluxus came about by accidents, too.

Warren Buffett insists he had no grand plan for Berkshire Hathaway, which made him one of the world's richest men. Buffett's company was a series of "happy accidents."

The history of food is filled with serendipity: saccharin, the microwave, cellophane, brown 'n serve rolls, Caesar salad, nachos, Wheaties, corn flakes. Overeat, and you might find a cure in another product of a happy accident: Alka-Seltzer. You actually could write an entire book about happy accidents just in the food industry alone, but you are too late. The book *How the Hot Dog Found Its Bun: Accidental Discoveries and Unexpected Inspirations That Shape What We Eat and Drink* by Josh Chetwynd beat you to it.

All of this brings to mind Kurt Vonnegut Jr.'s story of Eliot Rosewater. Young Eliot showed little talent for anything. Seeing this, his favorite uncle gave Eliot some life-changing advice: "A massive amount of money will change hands someday, son," the uncle said. "Get in the middle of it."

I nod each time I hear one of these stories. This book exists because I once wrote a book called *Selling the Invisible*—the result of at least three happy accidents.

Decades ago, I listened to a client debate a dozen ideas for growing his business. After a month of patient listening, I went to a printer and printed a button for him. The button had two words: *Do anything*.

I know it well: happy accidents are out there. You just need to get out in the middle of them. Because opportunity does not knock. People knock; opportunity answers.

Get out there.

Those Who Hesitate Are Lost

Several musicians who performed the premiere of Mozart's' *Don Giovanni* played with ink-stained hands. There was a good reason: Mozart had written the overture the night before, and the ink on the sheet music was still wet.

Herman Melville put off finishing *Moby-Dick* so often that, to ensure that he finished, he had his wife chain him to his writing desk.

But history's great procrastinators—Frank Lloyd Wright, Victor Hugo, and Bill Clinton, who Al Gore once kindly referred to as "punctually challenged"—are impulsive compared to planners. Left with the task of hatching a business plan, six of the seven people in the room will happily perch on the egg for months. It once prompted me to say, "Until I sat in on a strategic planning committee, I thought only the universe was infinite." Instead of plans, you get:

"We need more information."

"This hasn't been proven."

"No one has tried this."

"We tried something like this. It didn't work."

What stifles planning is our fear of doing. The doing may make our planning look foolish. So, rather than do, we keep planning.

You are likely to, too.

The problem is actually a pair: our fear of failure and our faith in perfection. This may be a pretty good plan, but is it perfect? Have we considered everything?

Seeking perfection, we sit.

But just as no person is perfect, no plan is, either. The idea isn't to perfect your plan and then act. The idea is to plan—and experience the rich learning that goes into it—and then execute the plan, refining as you go.

"No battle plan survives contact with the enemy," the war strategist Helmuth von Moltke famously said, to be echoed later by boxer Mike Tyson's observation about boxing: "Everyone has a plan until he gets punched in the face."

You put your plan in place, then adjust as the battle develops. You have to. Hatch a plan, act on it, and see how it survives the first punch in its face. Then adjust.

The path to perfection leads us to procrastination.

Just do it. Soon.

PERSUADING

Where Do You Begin?

In Kamloops, British Columbia, there is a lake that bears my family name. If you wonder if that lake and I are related, we are. The BC government named it after my dad to honor the hundreds of Kamloops trout he coaxed from it with flies that led back to his bamboo fly-fishing rod.

No fish was safe in a stream where my father was wading; he knew fish better than fish know fish. I recall the afternoon he pointed out to me, about thirty yards away, several flies fluttering in a beam of sunlight.

"There are three trout feeding there," he whispered. One cast and, seconds later, there were only two.

The great fishermen don't merely understand fishing; they understand fish. And the best marketers don't merely understand the tools of marketing; they understand whom they are trying to catch. They understand where their fish are swimming, how they think, and why they bite—and on what lures.

So the first key of marketing in this new world is perspective. Like dad understanding how fish think, you can work magic if you understand three things:

How do your prospects gather information about a service like yours?

How do they process that information?

And what makes them choose one service over another?

Let's go see.

How Service Prospects Think

Mistrust in the Age of Hype

I am standing paralyzed by too many choices of sweeteners at Starbucks—sugar, honey, and pink, blue, and yellow artificial sweeteners—when a flyer pinned to the bulletin board catches my attention.

It's for a writers workshop led by a "best-selling author." She has won nine international book awards.

Unaware of any international book awards, other than the Booker Prize for fiction, I check on her books on Goodreads and Amazon.

No one appears to have read them. There are four reviews, all on the same day.

I instantly think of another author's recent Facebook page post, touting his "number one Amazon bestseller." I look that book up, too. It does not exist; it's available only on audio and has not been released. And the author is not exactly the author, either; he was one of seventeen.

I email him. He replies that his book is the number one preordered business audiobook in its subcategory.

"So your audiobook is the bestseller among all the audiobooks in its category that have not been released?"

A day later, he replies: "If you put it that way, I guess so."

We live in an age of a million bestsellers, a million somethings that "will change (fill in the blank) forever"—in an age of unrelenting hyperbole.

You see this in the strange evolution of the word "unique." The word means the one and only. But it appears you can be even less than—or is it more than?—the one and only. Because we soon had the expression "the most unique," which soon wasn't praise enough and morphed into "truly the most unique" until it finally peaked at "truly the most unique X that I have ever seen in my entire life."

In the age of hype, we naturally have title inflation. In two of our country's premier management consulting firms, each person's title radiates authority. "Director" sounds very impressive—especially if you are a member of a board of directors, or a director of a film—until you learn there are "managing directors" everywhere. But those people, you discover, apparently are mere middle management because there are the even loftier "managing directors & partners." And even they toil a rung below "managing director & senior partner," and we have not even gotten to "president," of which the two firms no doubt have several.

My second profession, advertising, led this movement. In our Mad Men and Women vocabularies, the business cards of four in every ten employees read "vice president," and every product was new, but never merely new. They all were "All New and Improved!"—and always in capital letters. "Advertising," as Paul Valéry observed, "has annihilated the power of the most powerful adjectives."

We are in the Age of Hype. But alas, your prospects know this. And this dictates that your first communications task is not to overwhelm a prospect with your claims; it's to convince that person that you are worth listening to at all.

In the Age of Hype, the first thing you must earn is trust.

Schemes and Dreams and Circus Clowns

The internet almost roars with ideas for schemes that promise to "change your business forever." Read carefully, and you will not find a single example of one working. But the siege of claims makes you worry.

Don't. You are missing nothing.

General Motors thought it had a scheme for selling cars that people didn't want. They called them rebates. Within years, General Motors declared the most famous bankruptcy in American history. General Motors didn't need better schemes; they needed better cars. And when they started producing them, their revenues returned, too.

The enterprise that needs schemes to sell its services doesn't have a service. It has schemes.

Schemes are for Bernie Madoffs.

It's Not Rational

I started my advertising career on a tractor.

Figuring a copywriter who grew up in the land of Tillamook Cheese must know tractors, our creative director assigned me the Simplicity account.

It proved a rich opportunity. I got to write dealer songs with Dolly Parton jokes and to suggest that before you buy a Japanese garden tractor, you should take a long, sober look at a photo of a Japanese garden.

And I got my first startling lesson in how prospects think.

My predecessors had fashioned a compelling campaign. It compared a Simplicity tractor with the market-leading John Deere tractor, and invited prospects to compare. On point after point—at least thirteen—our tractor crushed the Deere.

But it didn't. Deere sales actually went up.

How could people resist our compelling argument? Fifteen years later, I stumbled on a book that helped explain it—and it changed forever how I think about marketing.

The book was *Inevitable Illusions* by Massimo Piattelli-Palmarini. And it essentially said that people often don't think, and for a good reason: it's often smarter not to think.

Why? Consider our origins: caves. A saber-tooth tiger suddenly appeared in our path. We had to react without thinking; he who thought for too long was dead.

Then there's a second fact that discourages us from thinking: our realization that thinking is hard work. If you ever heard the news that even great writers write for only three hours a day, you may have decided writing was a cushy job. It's not. I ran national-class marathons in my thirties, and writing takes far more effort. That's because, in writing, you have to think every single second. You spend most of the time in marathon, however, zoning out. Marathoning for two hours is easier than writing for three.

Thinking, quite simply, is very hard work.

And because we instinctively know that thinking taxes our reserves, we are smart about choosing when to think—and when not to.

We spend our thinking capital wisely.

Which means we regularly decide not to think too much. So, while there is an entire category of products known among marketers as "carefully considered purchases"—cars, televisions, and new homes comprise the Big Three—most purchases are not carefully considered.

And that was the problem with our Simplicity vs. Deere campaign. It asked buyers to sit and carefully consider thirteen different product features. It asked prospects to work hard. The prospects, however, just wanted to mow their lawns.

We think only when we must. In every other case, we decide. We are deliberately illogical.

And what does this mean for you?

You must present a case that allows prospects to decide fast. Ask them to go slow, and you are asking them to think hard. And that's too hard.

So don't give people thirteen good reasons, as Simplicity did. Give them one overwhelming one.

Don't make us think; help us decide. Quickly.

Think Fears, Not Desires

Product marketing focuses on satisfying our desires: to be more attractive, more admired, more healthy. Good service marketers, especially in this age of distrust, realize the more significant influence of fear.

We are fear-based. Maslow's famous hierarchy of needs recognizes this implicitly: we have to overcome our fear of not surviving at all, of being without food, clothing, and shelter before we can even consider our secondary needs.

You can see that we are fear-based from the famous studies on risk aversion. Essentially, they show that we feel the pain of losing twenty dollars far more acutely than we feel the pleasure of finding a twenty-dollar bill.

And one thing we particularly dread is making a wrong decision. This is partly ego, of course; a poor choice makes us feel foolish. Tests have shown, as a vivid example, that if faced with the choice of two different makes of strawberry jam, you will choose one, but if given five choices, you won't. You had only a 50 percent chance of making the wrong choice of the first but an 80 percent chance of the second.

So you leave the store jamless.

So, before you try to sell to prospects, ask yourself and your trusted advisors two questions:

What might my prospects fear about my service?

And what might assure them that I am a safe choice?

Don't focus solely on your prospects' desires. Identify their fears.

The Challenge: Stereotyping

In June 2015, the New England Patriots professional football team drafted defensive back Jordan Richards. Richards had played college football at Stanford, a college known to guidance counselors as the S in the elite HYPSM—Harvard, Yale, Princeton, Stanford, and MIT—of American colleges.

Richards impressed the Patriots' coaches from his first workouts, as captured in the *Boston Globe*'s first story on Jordan, posted August 4. 2015:

"When Richards was drafted, the book on him was that he is highly intelligent."

"'The thing that sticks out the most about him is he's a very smart guy,' fellow safety Devin McCourty said."

"'He's a smart kid and picks things up quickly,' coach Bill Belichick said."

Now, I first saw Richards play as a high school junior, and over thirty times since—and he is very intelligent. But he also weighs 211 pounds despite no more than 9 percent body fat, and—despite playing a position where speed is critical—sports a torso and two upper arms that appear overinflated. And, from a standing start, he can cover forty yards in just over 4.5 seconds. But what is the first thing you read about him?

Elite college grad Jordan Richards is smart.

The first thing we do when confronted with something new is to put it in a box. We categorize and label it and treat it accordingly. So players from Iowa are farm-tough, products from Germany are well engineered, clothes from Italy are stylish, and former ad copywriters from Minneapolis are "down-home jingle writers," a description that would make close friends roll on the floor in laughter.

But that is stereotyping, which we all do. Categorizing helps simplify our decisions—often in the wrong direction.

Accountants and engineers, therapists, insurance salesmen—everyone in business gets pigeonholed.

Early in my career, I led our presentation of a speculative campaign to the CMO for a computer monitor manufacturer. I feared that we faced a problem from the beginning: our agency president's infatuation with my background. He loved to tell people how this former Oregon lawyer and law review editor in chief had come all the way to Minneapolis to be part of his agency. And so, he made a point of stressing that to the client before I presented our recommendations.

But the presentation went wonderfully. The prospect raved about our campaign and our idea for the new brand name; he asked our CEO if he could purchase the rights to it.

And then he gave the business to Bozell.

Our baffled president called him. "But you thought our creative was the best of anyone—by far."

"I still do," the fellow answered.

"Then why didn't you give us the account?"

"Honestly, it's because Harry is a lawyer. And lawyers can't be creative."

So, to stereotype is human. It simplifies our choices, often too much. He saw a campaign that he thought was incredibly creative and then decided that it couldn't be: a lawyer had created it.

What could better illustrate the hold that our stereotypes have on us?

And these stereotypes are everywhere. Financial advisors are conservative white Republicans without senses of humor.

Models aren't very bright. (Cindy Crawford studied engineering at Northwestern on a full academic scholarship.)

Priests are compassionate. Professors live in ivory towers and are absentminded. Lawyers are just in it for the money. Accountants look at your shoes when they talk to you; actuaries look at their own shoes.

People stereotype you from their first impression of you and their stereotype of your industry. And those are two impressions you must overcome to win a prospect's confidence.

So, what are your prospects' stereotypes of you? Write them down. When you're done, write down what you need to say and do to overcome each of those first impressions.

And, as the "uncreative lawyer" example suggests, are there aspects of your background you should not reveal at all? Might they unfairly prejudice a prospect against you?

Overcome the wrong first impressions: your prospect's stereotype of you and your industry.

One Solution: Packaging Against Stereotype

In the days when advertising creative people dressed like artists on weekends, Tom McElligott stood out, most visibly for the audacious headlines that would land him, at just forty-seven years old, in the Advertising Hall of Fame. One vivid example was his headline for the Holy Bible on behalf of the Episcopal Church (Tom was the son of a preacher).

It read, "The Hero Gets Killed in the End."

Seeing these and other award-winning headlines, his agency's prospective clients almost certainly assumed Tom was another frustrated screenwriter, slumming in the ad biz for the art and the alcohol. These prospects arrived at the agency and were ushered upstairs, where they were introduced to the agency's head of accounting, naturally clad in a rep tie, a long-sleeved button-down shirt, his short hair neatly parted and his horned-rimmed glasses correcting his obvious nearsightedness.

The CPA, it turned out, was Tom.

There is no evidence that Tom, when he dressed each morning, was plotting to pull the wool over people's eyes. He was a true Midwesterner, so uncharacteristically unhip that he often referred to jeans as "dungarees." There is ample evidence, however, that Tom's packaging worked. Prospects assumed they would be getting an artist and ended up with someone who looked like a scientist who had cost-benefit-tested every headline he wrote. His personal packaging reassured them.

Venture capitalists in the Silicon Valley figured this out immediately. What's the stereotype of a VC? It's in the twist that people quickly put on that acronym: they called them "vulture capitalists." And everyone heard that they were getting fifty-five-foot-yacht rich. So how do VCs dress?

Show up at a meeting with one in a suit and tie and you will learn: What was I thinking? The VCs' shirts, slacks, and shoes are right off the rack from the Nordstrom in the Stanford Shopping Center. No ties, no Jaeger LeCoultre watches, no $400 shoes.

Just regular fellows, not getting rich, after all—it appears.

How might your prospects stereotype you?

The moment they meet you, how might you puncture that balloon?

Dress against your stereotype.

The Challenge: The Status Quo Bias

All service marketing implicitly asks its prospects to change. It asks them to seek help they have not sought before, or to switch from one provider to you.

So all marketing asks people to do something they dislike: change.

Our resistance is so strong that it's considered a cognitive bias and has earned a name: Status Quo Bias. However much we might dislike our current situation, we dislike even more the mere thought of changing. That's because we never get complete assurance that a change will be for the better. It might easily be for the worse.

There's another factor at work. Choosing you requires an effort, and using you requires even more. Maintaining the Status Quo, even an unpleasant one, requires no effort at all. In that sense, doing nothing offers more convenience.

So, your initial focus should not be, *How can I appear to be the superior choice?* It's, *How can I make changing look far more attractive to this person than staying the way they are?*

And once more, that's what John Deere did to our tractor. They became the Status Quo. For Simplicity to gain, it was going to have to do it by stealing business from Deere. But because Deere buyers were accustomed to Deere, we had to alter that Status Quo and get them to switch.

And like all of us, the Deere drivers were afraid to do that.

Don't merely sell yourself. Sell the rewards of changing the Status Quo.

Overcoming Status Quo Bias

Think again about products versus services like yours. Many products are necessities—food, clothing, shelter—and millions more are virtual necessities: toothpaste, soaps and detergents, cars, and the gasoline to run them.

By contrast, most services are actually luxuries. You can represent yourself in court; you can handle your own books and taxes; you can have friends shoot your wedding photos; you can cut your own hair. For years, as yet another example, businesses wishing to advertise had no need for an ad agency, because the publications and producers created the ads for the advertisers, or the advertisers created them themselves. And American businesses thrived for decades without management consultants like McKinsey, just as families both birthed and buried their own.

The difference in these two—a necessity versus a luxury—is critical. Selling a necessity is relatively simple, but selling a luxury takes courage, quality, capital, imagination, and luck. But let's skip four of those and focus on item four: imagination.

Your service looks like another luxury. *How might you make it look like a necessity?*

There's a drill for this. Imagine you are calling on a prospect who offers the objection, "Right now, your service really is a luxury for us. I'm not sure we can afford it."

How would you answer that? What is that prospect missing or misunderstanding?

"I understand. I used to think that, too. But let me explain."

What might make your service—or switching from another service to yours—a necessity?

The Challenge: Ambiguity Effects

I once observed a classic marketing challenge over the course of sixteen months. It involved something we all have: floors.

One of the first things I noticed on my first evening with Stephanie were three small sample blocks of wood on her granite kitchen counter.

"They're some floors I'm considering. I want to redo all these floors."

The blocks have moved several times in the eighteen months since then, and new blocks have joined them. Meanwhile, Stephanie wrestles with a famous cognitive bias: Ambiguity Effects. She cannot envision the result of changing. It's ambiguous to her.

She does not like her current carpeted floors but cannot clearly see the better alternative. And she's confronted by more options than she can process: six major brands, wood versus wool, synthetic, stain protection, pet pee protection, cost, and more combinations of colors and textures and patterns than—it makes my head hurt to think about it, too.

And she wonders if she might like some other floors more—even some not yet invented.

In product marketing, ambiguity bias only occurs in complex cases like Stephanie's one-hundred-floors-versus-five-hundred-carpets debate. No car buyer has to wonder how the new Camry might handle or accelerate, or how its bucket seats will feel. She can test the car and remove all doubt.

While in service marketing—selling the invisible, to coin a phrase—ambiguity bias is almost guaranteed. Your service doesn't even exist when a prospect considers it. It's merely a promise that you will do something later. So, while the car prospect can rely on his eyes, ears, and even nose, the service prospect must rely on faith.

The digital age has complicated this. Pre-internet, a prospect for a service knew there was a limit to the information he could gather. He might call and ask for brochures and ask a few friends, for example.

Today, by contrast, he knows there are Angie's List (now called Angi), Yelp reviews, rankings of service in many industries, dozens of websites, and hundreds of pages of articles on how to choose an investment advisor, for example.

In this Age of Over-information, a prospect afflicted with ambiguity bias might never act. He knows he can never get all the possible information. Or, just as bad, he fears he might decide without all that information, and quickly be afflicted with a problem you know well: buyer's remorse.

Again, this is your competition. It's not those who work in your niche. Instead, it's your prospect.

Overcome Ambiguity Effects.

Overcoming Ambiguity Effects

So, how do you overcome these Ambiguity Effects? How do you minimize a prospect's doubt?

Fitness clubs offer one way: CrossFit, Power Train, Snap Fitness, Anytime Fitness, and Gold's Gym all offer free trials. They're the equivalent of test drives. Divorce attorneys offer them, too: the free initial consultation.

There's a variation of this you can offer in advice services: the Opinion Letter. You can promote on your website, "Do you have a specific question for which you'd like a professional opinion? Send it to us and we'll reply."

If you can answer the question in twenty or fewer minutes, do so. If it will take longer, respond with, "The full answer to your question would require hours to answer. But here are some thoughts that might help you."

And, of course, this is what a first prospect meeting is intended to address. It's your prospect's chance to test-drive the relationship and see how it feels. It's all but indispensable, which in turn means that the driving force in all of your marketing is this:

Get a meeting.

Overcoming the Anchoring Effect

With only three exceptions, every startup that has come to me was anchored to shore.

Their anchors were the owner's perceptions of the business each startup was in.

They didn't have an idea for their enterprise; they had a template. The business card, the offices, the staffing and compensation model, and the media in which they advertised all looked the same.

Lawyers crave Greek columns, scales of justice, and Times New Roman type, always in black and never on a card stock farther from white than bone.

Wedding photographers want wedding bouquets displayed prominently somewhere, and everything bathed in a soft color and focus that whispers romance and hints at eternal love.

Health care services for seniors want photos of happy couples with senior hair and teenage skin—and strolling on a beach.

And every service wants artwork in the reception area that would neither interest nor offend anyone, but reassure each client that the company could afford art to cover its otherwise bare walls.

It's as if they want to convey to prospects, "Don't worry. We're not different. We're just like everyone else."

What drives this? Anchors. This is what businesses in their industry always have done. This is how they look. This is how we should look and act. We become anchored to those images.

Don't.

Watch your anchor.

The Challenge: Loss Aversion

All week of every week of football season, half of college football fans obsess over their team's loss. The fans of the winning teams stop celebrating Sunday and immediately start obsessing over their upcoming games. Losers remember.

Losers remember and obsess, while the winners forget and move on. Losses stick, but wins are forgotten. As ABC's *Wide World of Sports* used to remind all fans, victory is merely a thrill, but defeat is sheer agony.

Doug Sanders won twenty golf tournaments in his career and is remembered for his "Peacock of the Fairways" wardrobe—hundreds of pairs of shoes dyed to perfectly match the Crayola colors of his over two hundred pairs of slacks—and for the thirty-inch putt he missed to lose one tournament, the 1970 British Open.

Wins are nice. Losses are unforgettable.

For all of us, winning is nice but losing is agony. We are Jimmy Connors and Lance Armstrong and dozens of other athletes who have said exactly the same thing: "I hate to lose more than I love to win."

I've owned three laptop computers. One is sixteen years old and dead, a second one didn't survive the SUV that ran over it in a parking lot (long, sad story). But both of my laptops live on in my hall closet. They weren't cheap. So I don't want to lose them—despite the fact that both are old, neither works, and the MacBook I am typing this with right now works great. But I don't want to part with them, any more than you want to part with a dozen things hanging in your closet that you haven't worn in at least three years.

We hate to part with; we hate to lose.

We love wins, but we loathe losses—more than twice as much, according to a famous study by the Nobel Prize–winning economist Daniel Kahneman.

Your prospects hate losses more than they love wins: they fear pain more than they covet gain.

So, never mind what gain you can offer your prospect for a moment. *What loss can you help your prospect avoid?*

Sell a Painkiller, Not a Vitamin

You see it everywhere you look: Sell benefits, not features.

The typical positioning statement instructs you to tell your point of difference and its benefit to your prospects. (I plead guilty. I was younger then.) Everyone became anchored to benefits. We all missed what should have been apparent, if we simply looked inside ourselves.

The Buddhists, and every expert on motivation, realize that we have four matched sets of primary desires. The first set is the desire to find pleasure, and to avoid pain. Marketers, however, have trouble thinking of avoiding pain as a benefit. A painkiller doesn't make your life better, after all. It just returns it to normal.

So "benefits" thinking drove marketers to a standard list of benefits.

You will earn more money.

You will look more attractive.

You will get better mileage. Or faster acceleration.

You will get the girl.

What is missing here? *It's that while people enjoy pleasure, they hate pain far more than they enjoy pleasure.* When I am in pain, I don't stand in the drugstore wondering if the Advil costs too much, or whether I should just forget it and go home. I don't desire the Advil—I need it.

When you sell benefits, you are selling nice-to-haves. When you are selling pain avoidance, you are selling must-haves. Which is easier?

Put this in a context: financial planners. The typical financial planner assures you that while nothing is certain—even bonds have failed, after all—"you can reasonably expect a good return on your investment with a balanced portfolio of stocks and bonds. You probably will be better off next year than you are now."

How compelling is that?

What if you switched from a benefit focus to a loss-avoidance focus?

"If you fail to invest, you will lose immediately, because the current rate of inflation means your money will be worth less in a year than it is today. You will have less real spending power. Plus, every signal suggests the market should rise 6 to 7 percent this year. If you fail to capture that gain, you will effectively lose $14,000 over the course of this year—which is almost $300 every week."

Another common example: The fitness instructor approaches a fifty-five-year-old male client who is considering personal training.

The trainer can promise to make the client stronger. Or she can tell the client that, like every man his age, he is losing mass every year. Unless he exercises, his shoulders and arms will get smaller and weaker, which translates to losses.

To the typical man, as everyone knows, size matters. So, what is more apt to get him to sign up?

So, when you draft your Target, Evidence, and Claim statements, don't think of benefits. Think first about losses: What losses can you prevent?

What pain can you help a client avoid?

As the venture capitalists say, "We're not interested if you are selling vitamins. Vitamins just promise to make people healthier. But if you have a painkiller, we're in. It's much easier to sell a painkiller."

Think about the benefit of working with you—but particularly the pain you can kill and the losses you can prevent.

The Ultimate Pain Reliever Campaign

For inspiration on addressing your prospect's fear of loss, there is one brilliant model: Crispin Porter Bogusky's award-winning 2006 "Safe Happens" campaign for Volkswagen.

Shot documentary style, each of the campaign's commercials open on a driver and front-seat passenger chatting amiably as they drive on an everyday city street. Just as you wonder where this story is going, your view out the car window shakes to shocking sounds of car metal against car metal and shattering window glass.

The screen briefly goes blank. It evokes your fear of the ultimate loss, death.

Now you see the driver and passenger standing outside the car, surveying the damage. Just as you and I might, the driver utters the commercial's final spoken words: "Holy sh—"

And then, the evidence: "Highest Government Safety Rating."

What car crash can you save your prospective clients from?

What loss do your prospects and clients fear?

Leveraging the Peak End Rule

Each of these three examples illustrates an important rule for every aspiring persuader:

1. Fans of football teams with 10-2 records that win their bowl games feel happier after the season than fans of 11-1 teams who lose their bowl games.
2. We save desserts for the end of our meals.
3. And if the server leaves us a piece of candy with the check, we tip an average of 15 to 20 percent more.

Each of these is yet another illustration of the Peak End Rule. This describes the fact that people do not remember and assess their experiences by the entire experience. Instead, people remember an experience for how it felt at its peak—its best or worst—and at its end.

The football fans' memory of the End—the bowl game that ends each season—colors their view of the entire season. The bowl game winners with 9-3 season records actually feel happier than the bowl game losers with 11-1 records—a seemingly better season.

And your prospects and clients remember how you finish—the first meeting, your presentation, and each engagement—vividly, too.

The Peak End Rule applies to every key marketing moment: every presentation and prospect meeting and every marketing communication. And this book will offer several suggestions for ending well. But for now, ask: How strongly are you ending your emails? Your prospect meetings? Your presentations?

End well. It makes all the difference.

Leveraging Bandwagon Effects

In 2012, presidential candidates spent over 51 million dollars campaigning in Iowa. The Republicans alone spent over 500 days—over 16 months—combing the state, a state with only 6 of our nation's 538 total electoral votes.

They spent all that shoe leather and millions just to "win Iowa"?

No. They did it to win the nomination. As students of marketing campaigns, they understand Bandwagon Effects, a term that actually comes from a presidential campaign. In 1848, a nationally famous circus clown named Dan Rice—he invented the modern circus by blending animal acts, acrobats, and clowns—loved candidate Zachary Taylor and began touring on Taylor's behalf in his circus wagon. "Jump on the bandwagon," the clown urged voters, and they jumped. Taylor, a general with no formal education, won the election.

Candidates swarm all over Iowa, and in New Hampshire a week later, because they know that winning a million Iowans can make them look like the choice of over one hundred million Americans.

Publishers understand bandwagons. They press to get their books on bestseller lists, knowing other readers will see the lists and decide, "If so many people bought it, it must be good."

And movie studios and television networks try to trigger Bandwagon Effects by publicizing each week's list of top-grossing movies and highest-rated programs. Get on the bandwagon, they are saying.

Can you generate a Bandwagon Effect?

Client lists can do that. If notable clients are on our bandwagon, it's safe and smart to jump aboard.

Your growth chart can generate a Bandwagon Effect. "We're growing 15 percent annually," the chart shows. "People are jumping aboard."

And just looking successful evokes a Bandwagon Effect. If you appear successful, I assume clients are coming to you. Knowing people are joining your bandwagon makes prospects feel more comfortable about leaping on with them.

What are all the ways you can show your prospects your bandwagon?

Leveraging the Mere Exposure Effect

In the ten years ending in 2000, the thirty companies that made up the Dow Jones Industrial Average generated a 309 percent average return on investment.

The five hundred companies that comprise the Standard & Poor's 500 returned 308 percent.

The thirty companies with America's best-known brands? Four hundred and two percent.

In a famous study, people were shown dozens of photos of people they had never seen before. Later, they met these people and were asked which people they liked most.

They liked the ones whose photos they had seen most often.

Researchers in another famous study exposed people to meaningless Chinese characters. Later, these people were shown the same Chinese characters and several new ones. Which characters did the subjects like most and think conveyed the most positive connotations?

They were the symbols they already were familiar with. It's called the Mere Exposure Effect, and it could not have been more vivid than in the early stages of the 2016 presidential election. Who were the best-known names in the respective races?

1.   The former first lady of the United States, as well as secretary of state, and author of a best-selling book, *It Takes a Village*;

2.   The youngest son of the man who was our vice president or president for twelve years (1981–1993), as well as being the

younger brother of the man who was our president for an additional eight years (2001–2009); and

3. A man who for a combined eleven years hosted two major network TV programs, *The Apprentice* and *Celebrity Apprentice*; had authored five top-selling books on business, all in which his name appears in larger and bolder type than the book titles; has appeared in several television series or movies; and whose name at this writing appears on twenty-one different products and services, including menswear, cologne, and one of New York City's most visible buildings.

On September 1, 2015, these three people were not merely leading in the polls for their parties' nominations; they led by massive amounts. These massive leads seemed in perfect sync with their leads in name familiarity; the two brand names in American politics and one of a handful of the top brand names in American businesses. If the Mere Exposure Effect did not explain their leads entirely, can anyone possibly dismiss the fact that it was doing just what it says: having an effect?

Familiarity breeds contempt? Only far too much of it. The best-known brands, the familiar faces, and the more familiar Chinese characters are among the convincing proof for a key principle in marketing:

Familiarity breeds regard. To know of you, with few exceptions, is to like you.

By every means possible, make your name more familiar.

But Forget Branding (Honest)

For many years when I preached the power of branding, the partners in the client firms—accountants, lawyers, wealth managers—often would wince. The idea that accountants were like automobiles seemed ridiculous to them.

They were right, mostly.

My doubts about service brands started one afternoon in Istanbul in 2005. Three young Turks—literally—were discussing love brands in the presentation before mine. Turks seem excited about love brands; it felt like some Turkish revival meeting. And what do I remember about sitting there?

I remember squirming. Something felt wrong. I couldn't think of any service that reasonably could be called a "love brand." I felt like those accountants and lawyers.

Are there product love brands? Heavens, I can start at my feet and work up, and name four: Puma driving sneakers, H&M boxer briefs, Athleta workout shorts, and Under Armour nylon shells. I am right this minute staring into my ultimate love brand: an Apple laptop.

But my service love brands? It took me ninety seconds to think of one: Megan Flaherty. She works for Spalon Montage and cuts my hair. Do I love Spalon Montage? I can't; I don't even know them. Spalon Montage doesn't cut my hair. This person does.

Do Accenture's clients love Accenture? How could they? Accenture doesn't advise them; some people there do.

What's Accenture, or any other service? Most vividly, it's not one thing. It's an assortment. And the assortment changes as some people come and others go.

Similarly, what is a large law firm? It depends on with whom you work. How good is it? That depends, too. They may be renowned for litigation, but you hear their IT practice is weak and their labor-law group is new. And one of their antitrust stars left to become a federal judge.

In a sense, there is no law firm. It's mostly a roof for several hundred different services and service providers.

So, are there any true service brands? In consulting, McKinsey and Bain have true, deep brands; so do Kleiner Perkins, Sequoia Capital, and Andreessen Horowitz in venture capital; Fidelity, Vanguard, and American Funds in mutual funds; Grey, Wieden

+ Kennedy, BBDO, and Ogilvy in advertising; and Skadden, Arps, Jones Day, Baker McKenzie, and Kirkland & Ellis in law, along with niche brands such as Littler in labor law. But those are a few firms among millions.

And what do these brands have in common? Sheer mass—their names are constantly in the news. Every day, clients for these firms read about them. The huge firms have brands because their names are everywhere their prospects look.

Brands appear to observe the Law of Five (Plus or Minus Two). We have limited room in our brains for brands in any category. Three to five achieve brand stature; the rest only make impressions.

A service marketer's task, then, is not to build the brand. Your task is to achieve the many impressions that create name familiarity.

Familiarity first, then impression, even eventually a reputation. But brands? Brands are for the behemoths.

The Branding Fallacy

I will take some of the blame.

My relentless championing of branding in my first three books may have helped inspire many people to conclude two things: Branding is the key to marketing success. And you, too, can become a brand.

I think of Istanbul, where a panel of four followed my presentation by gushing—for what seemed an hour—on aforementioned "love brands." ("Love brands" is actually a concocted term, popular in the first decade of the century, for adored brands like Apple and Nike.)

You, too, the panel suggested to the audience of small to mid-sized businesses, can become a brand.

But branding is not the key to your business's success. The number of bona fide brands on this planet probably cannot exceed five hundred—and there are 7.9 billion people on Earth.

Which puts your odds of achieving brandom at over 150 million to one.

So, what should you aspire to instead?

"I've-heard-of-you-ness."

Virtually everyone who has heard of your business will assume, from that alone, that you are more skilled than any business less familiar.

You cannot, in the next ten years, become a brand. But you can look, sound, and seem familiar. How?

By imprinting in people's minds a distinctive name, look, and voice.

And how might you do that?

We'll explore that in the next section.

Maximize your *"I've-heard-of-you-ness."*

Our Brand Does What?

Your "brand" doesn't do anything.

You do.

If you focus on your brand, you take your eyes off the ball.

A Reminder About Marketing's Clichés

World-class?

A commitment to excellence?

Decades of experience solving our clients' problems?

You have heard all of that before.

If you've read it in someone else's sales pitch, don't put it in yours.

Is What You Are Saying Invaluable?

If you post something online, in the hope at least one key prospect will respond to it, at least one person has to spend their most valuable asset, their time, to read and respond to you.

So before you post anything, ask:

Is this information so valuable that someone will read it—and become more inclined to use your services?

When you post information online, you are competing with all the information out there. Does yours distinguish itself?

Or are you just writing in the hope that it might?

Communicate only something important.

The Most Powerful Word in Persuasion

Because our greatest interest is in ourselves, "you" is the most powerful word in persuasion.

"You're in good hands with Allstate."

"Let your fingers do the walking through the Yellow Pages."

"When you care enough to send the very best."

The most compelling headline yet written illustrates this: "You are not alone."

"Because you're worth it."

Use the word "you."

Your Name

Your First Step Is Huge

If it weren't for my name, I might be anonymous.
—Jethro Pugh, 1944–2015, Dallas Cowboys, 1965–78

Walking to work today, I passed a sign that stuck out to me, for all the wrong reasons.

The sign read: "Finished Basement Company."

I immediately was reminded of a young therapist who earlier this week came to me for advice. I remembered her because I'd met her several times before. But if someone asked me to look up the name of her fledgling therapy business, I would have had no idea.

That's because it had a name similar to Finished Basement Company. It was too long and too generic to remember.

And in this new world of massive competition for attention, a name like that suggests a death wish.

Names really matter. You want people to remember you, and to call. But they can neither remember nor will they call an utterly forgettable name.

One of my first clients created software. The company was backed by venture capitalists, one of whom attended my initial meeting with the client. After some preliminaries, he stood and said something that stuck with me forever.

"The first two things a prospect uses to judge you is your name and your price," he said.

"We have to get those right first."

You do, too. It's a step that can literally hurl you forward, or all but glue you to the ground. Take naming your business very seriously.

Choose a name that can become familiar fast.

P.S. This naming experience was telling for another reason. That little software company, my first client, became Macromedia, which is now part of Adobe, a merger that netted MacroMedia $3.4 billion. The name really did matter.

A Reminder: The Power of a Unique Name

There are six peaks in Europe taller than the Matterhorn.

Name one.

Choose a memorable name.

Think Like a Singer

Think of Madonna, Rihanna, Adele.

How many times did you hear their names before you remembered them? Not more than twice.

The people who market singers have known this forever: choose a name that people remember almost instantly. (Fortunately, Madonna and Adele were given those memorable names at birth, and Rihanna is that singer's given middle name.)

We hear these names three times and think, *I keep hearing about her. She must be worth listening to.*

We assume if everyone is remarking about something, it must be remarkable.

So, decades ago, there was Elvis, Fabian, and Dion. Plus a guy named Fats, a band apparently named for some insects—The Beatles— and another named for rocks rolling down a hill.

We choose the things that seem familiar, and what others choose. People are aboard your bandwagon. We want on, too.

Knowing this, would you ever name a therapy service Jonathan Walter Counseling?

Or a childcare center Northwest Childcare Center?

Or a studio Pinnacle Photographic Services?

Would you ever choose a name that no one can remember, rather than one no one can forget?

Think like a singer. Choose an easily remembered name.

It's Like Naming a Child

Twenty-five years ago, every good-sized town had three copy shops. You don't need to check old Yellow Pages to know the names they chose.

There was a FastPrints, a QuickPrints, and an InstyPrints. No one could tell them apart and people who saw a FastPrints thought it was for something called InstaPrints and called InstyPrints instead. Everyone ended up effectively marketing everyone else.

Every Smith knows better than to name their son John. If you are a parent, in fact, you probably labored for weeks choosing a distinctive name for your children.

And now we have a world of Cole and Cooper Beckwiths, and London and Ireland McGregors, and one Equanimeous St. Brown (a former wide receiver for Notre Dame).

You instinctively know the value of a distinctive name for your children. Apply that thinking to your business; you want it to thrive, too.

Sweat your name.

But Naming It After You?

Shouldn't I just name my business after myself?

I once thought so; I was new to this. Plus, there weren't many Beckwiths, so that meant the business name Beckwith was short, relevant, and relatively unusual—a Near-Perfect Three.

But your name probably isn't unusual. And when you decide to retire, your name won't be relevant because you no longer are providing the service. Where, for five examples, are Mr. Ogilvy, Mr. Peat or Mr. Marwick, and Mr. Skadden or Mr. Arps?

Years from now, your name will sound old, and the prospects for your successor company will want the most current thinking. In our new world of overnight innovation, it's much better to be Mr. Tesla than Mr. Ford.

As a vivid illustration, consider the cautionary tale of the car named for Mr. Olds.

In 1901, Ransom Olds produced our country's first mass-produced car. For years, it led the industry in sales. In 1976, in fact, more Americans bought an Oldsmobile Cutlass than purchased any other car. But the Olds car's fall came quickly and, in 1988, the marketers tried to break that fall with a campaign that insisted, "This is not your father's Oldsmobile."

We weren't convinced. Just sixteen years later, the Oldsmobile died. It was only 107 years old.

Your name is not merely a bow on the package; it's the wrapping paper. And like all things, names get old fast. Think carefully before you put yours on your business.

The best name for your business probably isn't yours.

Mavs and Cavs and Bonos and Becks

For decades, fans watched the New York Knickerbockers. Then they decided that name was too much work.

It's now the Knicks.

And think of how often they're just Mavs (Mavericks), Cavs (Cavaliers), and Jags (Jaguars). Or, in what may seem a stranger abbreviation, "Niners" and rarely the four-syllable Forty-Niners.

And it's Tiger, J-Lo, Beck and Bono, and Fergie. It's Sting, Prince, and Kobe. And it's Queen, Rush, and Heart. And The Stones—Rolling Stones takes too long—just as golf fans call their young star simply Rory.

What's going on here? George A. Miller helped us figure this out, and then produced a landmark paper to explain it.

To understand Miller's discovery, try this. Read the following:

Apple, omelette, Elvis.

Now close your eyes and repeat what you just read. So far, so good. Now try:

Pancakes, sweatshirt, sapphire, navy, bible, napkin, dishwasher.

If you recited that list back, you are Jerry Lucas, the NBA Hall of Fame basketball star and Phi Beta Kappa graduate of Ohio State. Lucas, who wrote thirty books on memory, could read a page of a phone book and recite it verbatim. But for the rest of us, Miller coined a rule as part of the most cited papers in psychology: "the Magic Rule of Seven, Plus or Minus Two."

Miller found that you and I can recall not more than seven "chunks" of information. To be helpfully specific: We can recall five words, six letters, and seven digits. We can remember our friends' seven-digit phone numbers if we need to, but if asked to include the area code we're lost.

For the same reason, if the television show had been called *Beverly Hills 90210-0803*, our only hope for getting the number right would be to call Jerry Lucas.

Can we remember the name Facebook? It's easy. It's only two chunks, "Face" and "book." The same thinking—mashups of two words into one—prompted the naming of Netflix, YouTube, PayPal, Pinterest, and SoulCycle.

Now this revealing test. Everyone in my adopted city remembers the restaurant named 110 Groveland, which has twelve characters. But almost no one would remember it if it was 605 Groveland Arch.

Why?

It's because the second name is not merely four letters longer than the first; *it's two chunks longer.* 110 Groveland takes four chunks: One Ten Grove Land. The second takes six: Six Oh Five Grove Land Arch. That's 50 percent more to try to recall. Few of us can.

You create another challenge if you choose a long name. We know our memory's limits. When we see something that we know exceeds it, we don't try to record the name; we know we are foolish to try. For the same reason, it's a rare person like Jerry Lucas who even tries to remember the names of four people to whom they are introduced at once.

We don't try to do what we can't. So try for not more than three chunks.

Make it short.

Name Like the Billionaires Do

It's clear the venture capitalists and angel investors that invested their billions in Silicon Valley were aware of Miller's implicit advice on naming a company.

Take a look at this Silicon Valley stars list:

Netflix, Spotify, Twitter, Mozilla, and YouTube? Seven characters.

Google, PayPal, Yahoo!, and Safari? Six.

Apple, Adobe, Pixar, Skype, and Tesla? Five.

Tivo, Uber, Hulu, and eBay? Four.

And then consider these other stars of the New Economy: Nike, Target, Costco, Cisco, Sun, Oracle.

And consider, too, Old Economy companies like Minnesota Mining and Manufacturing, Harley-Davidson, International Business Machines, Federal Express, Saks Fifth Avenue, and Sears & Roebuck. What are they now?

They're 3M, Harley, IBM, FedEx, Saks, and Sears.

What's the longest name above? There are actually four, because you measure the length of a name by the time it takes to say it.

Spotify, Safari, Mozilla, and IBM each has three syllables. The other twenty-six have only one or two.

Perhaps yours should, too.

Make it even shorter.

Surprise!

Nothing gives you a jolt like being caught by surprise. A surprising name has the same effect: it jolts people to attention.

Absolute wouldn't be a great name for a vodka. But because no one expects what seems to be a misspelled name, Absolut works. Plus, the name makes the vodka sound imported, which it is: from Sweden.

Toy Are Us would be a good name for a toy store, because people cannot literally be toys. But Toys "R" Us is even more unexpected and it even has a twist: the "R" is backward.

Virgin Airlines' name surprises you. Why the name? It came from a meeting where founder Richard Branson joked about the sheer audacity of his entire idea.

"What do we know about airlines?" he said. "We're virgins at this."

You may not want to appear surprising, of course; you might be a large accounting firm for Fortune 500 companies and decide a name like Kazoo! won't play well. But even here, notice how one of the world's biggest consulting firms introduced an element of surprise: PricewaterhouseCoopers.

And surprising doesn't have to mean audacious; it can simply be something no one else has done, as Minnesota Mining and Manufacturing did. They became a number and a letter, 3M, an unexpected combination—and lightning fast as a needed bonus.

Go for surprise: choose an unexpected name.

Be the Marble, Not the Pebble

Toss a shiny red marble on a beach some time and look around to see what happens.

No one notices all the pebbles, but people stop and point at your marble.

Names work exactly the same way.

The Relevant Name

Several years ago, the Denver-based international engineering consulting firm MWH invited me to speak and consult with them. I could not miss their first problem: it was seven emails before I could remember their name.

MWH specializes in water projects, like wastewater treatment plants, water filtration plants, and dams around the world—in thirty-five countries at the latest count. But their name did not suggest any of that; it suggested nothing. What name would be better to suggest a global company that dealt with water?

I suggested Blue Globe: water, international, a hint of their passion for the environment, in two syllables, and a name you could picture: a blue globe.

Consider this when you consider your name: What might you say—in an unexpected way—that will capture your essence just in your name alone?

Use your name to communicate something unexpected but relevant.

Adventures in Relevance

The name Google is relevant: you can find a googol of information by using Google.

Yahoo! is relevant. It's like Eureka!—Greek for "I have found it"—and refers to the excitement of finding something you were looking for.

Adidas sounds contrived to some. But it's an abbreviation of the name of the company's founder, Adi Dassler.

Chipotle, a smoked hot chili pepper used in Mexican cooking, suggests "Mexican cuisine."

Skype? It lets you fly through the sky to talk to someone. (The name comes from "Sky Peer-to-Peer.")

Twitter? The dictionary says it means, "A short burst of inconsequential information."

Write down your key messages, like MWH's key messages: "international," "water specialists," and "socially and environmentally conscious."

Then build your name around those relevant elements.

Tell us something that means something.

Change of Name, Change of Fortune

Shortly before *Selling the Invisible* appeared, my phone rang.

It was Stephanie Prem, the marketing director of the wealth management division of Norwest (later Wells Fargo). She'd read my *Selling the Invisible* article in *Twin Cities Business*.

And she wanted me to come and share its ideas with her fellow principals.

The presentation went well. Well enough, it turned out, that managing partners Peter Glanville and Stephanie asked if I would advise them on a new marketing campaign.

I already felt comfortable enough with these two engaging people to express myself frankly, so I said I would help them on one condition.

"And what is the condition?" Peter asked.

"You have to change your name."

The division was operating as Norwest Capital Advisors. I carefully laid out for them all the reasons that their name would make my job too hard.

First, Norwest is a bank. Banks do not offer significant returns on their depositors' investments. Plant your savings in one and they will award you with what was then a 3 percent annual return. Meanwhile, the average Fortune 500 company stock had produced an average 10.5 percent annual return. That return, and not savings account returns, is what a wealth management client wants.

Second, banks do not provide intense personal service. You stand in a line. The teller smiles, handles your transaction, and sends you on your way. That's fine for a bank. But it's intolerable in a wealth management service, not least of all because wealthy clients are used to having their hands—and doors—held.

Third, businesses have capital. Individuals have assets. A "capital advisor," if it means anything, means a business advisor.

And fourth, as you already know from reading the section before this, the name Norwest Capital Advisor is far too long. It's closer to being a sentence than a name. "Four syllables are all you get," I told Peter and Stephanie. "You used those up before you got to 'Advisors.'"

I went into action. Three weeks later, I presented my recommendation to the group. "I think you should rename your business Lowry Hill."

The name "Lowry" carried meaning in the Twin Cities. Thomas Lowry was one of the city's founding fathers, the man behind its original streetcar lines, and the man for whom the area near Lake of the Isles is named, a zip code filled with large homes and affluent citizens.

"Hill" carried another connotation. The wealth in many large metro areas is concentrated in an area called Hill, not least of all because families who can afford large homes love nice views. Boston has Beacon Hill, Chestnut Hill, and Fisher Hill; San Francisco has Nob Hill; Atlanta has Brookwood Hills; Dallas has Westover Hills; and Portland has West Hills.

Even my tiny hamlet had one, where all the doctors in the north part of our county lived. The locals referred to it as Pill Hill.

Eight years later, I was at a Lowry Hill retreat and learned that the group now was managing $6.6 billion in assets, a sixfold increase over those eight years. After dinner that night, I approached Stephanie and asked what they had done to grow so dramatically.

"We changed our name and advertised more. That's it. Getting a memorable name and promoting it had even more impact than you promised."

What's in a name? Maybe millions.

Your Message

Little Things Aren't

The more similar two services seem, the more important each tiny difference.

Accentuate the seemingly trivial.

Communicate What You've Done, Not What You Can Do

What demonstrates your ability to perform? DecisionQuest's research on millions of jurors provides one answer:

"Jurors look at actual achievements, lawyers look at credentials."

It makes sense. Earning an impressive degree from a well-regarded university or publishing an article in a respected publication offers hints that you might be able to perform. But actual performance proves it.

Your prospects think like jurors in the courtroom. They know that knowing and doing are two different things. If know-how mattered most, America's best golf instructors—David Leadbetter, Hank Haney, and Butch Harmon—each would have succeeded in professional golf. But Ledbetter never qualified for the PGA tour, Haney did not bother to try, and Harmon quit the tour after qualifying for only one of golf's four major tournaments, the 1970 US Open, and then failed to qualify for the final two rounds.

Stress your performance, not your credentials.

Telling Versus Selling

When you feel that you are being sold, you push back.

If people feel that by looking at your website, they push back.

Tell, don't sell.

Selling doesn't work on you, or anyone else. Telling does.

The Lesson That Changed My Life

In 1988, the editor of a small Minneapolis magazine praised the draft of an article that I'd submitted to him. But he offered one suggestion.

"Don't tell people what to do. Tell them stories instead."

Since that afternoon, on paper and behind podiums, I follow Steve Kaplan's advice. I tell stories.

I have two reasons for this. I want people to follow my suggestions and remember those suggestions after I've spoken. So I search for stories that surprise people, because surprises grab people's attention and lodge in their memories. One never forgets, as a vivid example, the Oscar Mayer Wienermobile.

We crave stories from birth. Listen for the first two-syllable words that a child learns. "Mommy" and "Daddy" come first. If the parents own a dog, "Doggie" comes next. Otherwise, the child's third complex word is "story." But of course.

Stories teach us how everything works.

A storyteller never tries to tip off the ending, and you shouldn't either. You need that suspense. And you want the audience members to learn your story's lesson on their own. This approach reflects a basic trait: we most strongly believe our own conclusions. Foist one on us, and we resist.

A famous test captured our enormous self-confidence in our own knowledge. People were asked a dozen questions and then rated their confidence in each of their answers. What do these tests tell us about total confidence?

When people report they are 100 percent confident in their spelling of a word, as one example, they are wrong 20 percent of the time!

So, if you want to persuade someone, take my editor's advice. Don't start with your conclusion. People will tend not to believe it anyway. And because giving your conclusion ends any suspense, they will stop listening.

Instead, tell them a story that leads them to the conclusion on their own.

They then will own the conclusion. And people hate to surrender anything they own.

Learn from a child. Tell stories.

The Heart Is the Heart of the Matter

Remember all those silly car ads?

The pages after magazine pages featuring a leggy blonde supine upon the polished curves of the new 1979 whatever-mobile?

These ads still appear, of course. Dos Equis's popular "Most Interesting Man in the World" commercials always end with a shot of the Mr. No Feminine Side seated at a restaurant table and surrounded by the former Miss Some State, perhaps spoofing Hugh Hefner.

Many argue that these ads imply a deceptive promise: buy this product and the hottie comes free.

But that isn't the creators' intent. These ads use the same device used by advertisers who engage cute babies or puppies to disarm us. Think of Flo for Progressive insurance.

When we see these commercials, we don't assume the products advertised come with a street-smart infant, a Holstein cow, or a charming Labradoodle. The ads use those devices to create an emotional association and elevate our mental state. (It's also why many ads use humor and smiling people.) Later, when we are exposed to that product, we feel something positive.

We don't know why. We might not even be conscious of the feeling.

But it happens.

Creatives regularly rail against this practice, condemning these ads for relying on "borrowed interest." But what the borrowers really are lifting is an emotional context.

They realize we buy with our hearts.

This also explains why the only ads that feature cats are ads for cat products. For reasons beyond the scope of this entry, many people—particularly men—don't like cats. (As one piece of evidence: according to Google's Ngram Viewer, books published since 1950 have used the word "dog" twenty-five times more often than the word "cat.")

Advertisers realize that they cannot easily deliver a message that alters our opinion of a product. But in just thirty seconds, they can leave us with a feeling.

Later, when we are exposed to the product, we revive that feeling. We smile at the Chick-fil-A sign because the cow makes us smile. We smile at the thought of E-Trade—even though we suspect that diaper-clad kid will grow up to be an intolerable wiseass. We smile at the Travelers' umbrella, because the anxious dog with his bone engaged us from beginning to peaceful end.

We even associate a car with an attractive person, and it becomes more attractive to us.

We buy, time and again, with our feelings.

And so advertisers evoke those feelings, with former pageant winners, cute cows, and "troubled" insomniac Labradoodles.

See? You're smiling just thinking about him.

Give your message emotional resonance. Make them feel the results. Tell them stories of others you've helped that have not just a result, but an emotional element—how did that person feel—and therefore, how might that prospect feel.

Reach hearts. Your prospects may think with their heads, but they buy with their hearts.

How to Be Fascinating

The second most interesting thing you can communicate: say something new.

The third most interesting thing you can communicate: say something in a way we have not heard before.

And the most interesting thing you can say?

Say something new, in a way we have not heard before.

What's in a Word?

Call someone you care about today."

"Achieve everything you are capable of."

Stop for a second.

Do you recognize those slogans?

Those are the messages in two of the world's most famous slogans: AT&T's "Reach Out and Touch Someone," and the US Army's "Be All You Can Be."

None of those two statements would ever have worked. They sound commonplace; you've heard them before. These famous slogans say the same thing, yet they affect us differently.

For years, they were known as gravitationally completely collapsed objects, and only physicists talked about them. Then some clever physicist gave them another name, and everyone was talking about them.

He called them "black holes."

Avis could not compete with Hertz. It was second only to it, but a far distant second. And then an agency recommended six words that made the business explode.

He recommended, "We're Number Two; We Try Harder."

John Caples wrote one of his many famous direct mail pieces and got another strong response. He decided to change just one of the ad's words among hundreds, and 20 percent more readers answered the ad.

He changed "repair" to "fix."

What's in a word? Sometimes, everything. Sometimes, the word you choose is the difference between being unknown and being a phenomenon.

Choose your words wisely.

Communicating

Mt. Everest is 29,000 feet high.

Most sites say it's twenty-eight feet taller.

It isn't. But when the first measurements were done, the surveyors realized that if they listed "29,000 feet" as the mountain's actual height, no one would trust the number.

So they unrounded the number up.

Most people don't trust suspiciously round numbers in marketing materials. "We increased their business 25 percent" sounds suspicious, or like a guess, and even a cliché.

Think about it. You rarely read 21, 23, 24, or 26 percent. It's always 25. *To be trusted, be specific.*

The Challenge: Resisting "the Best" Temptation

The first and overwhelming impression that every marketer begins with is the belief that your primary task is to distinguish yourself from your competitors.

You need to position yourself against your competition. And you need to appear to be the superior choice.

So let's test that hypothesis, just as I often do with students and other audiences for my presentations.

I will ask the audience, "How many of you use babysitters, at least occasionally?"

I will then pick out someone—a smiling face, of course—and begin a discussion that proceeds as follows.

"Now where do you live?"

"Atlanta," she responds.

"What area?"

"Ansley Park."

"Ahh, it's beautiful. Now, you often use babysitters. Do you have one in particular that you favor?"

"Yes. Ashley."

"Ashley from Ansley. Nice branding on her part!"

A chuckle.

"Now, is Ashley the best babysitter in Ansley Park?"

"The best?"

"Yes. The best."

"Gosh, I'm not sure."

"You're not sure that you are entrusting your little Madison to the best babysitter in Ashley Park?"

"I guess, well, not."

"You spent nine months carrying her, endured morning sickness, and the this-feels-like-the-Exorcist pain of childbirth to bring this precious gift into life, and you're not sure she's getting the best possible care in Ansley Park?" (I say this with a smile, of course.)

"I guess not. But Ashley is very good."

"Of course she is. You wouldn't choose less than very good. But tell me, how much time might you and your husband take if someone suggested to you the three best babysitters in your area?"

"I actually might spend two weeks."

"And your husband?" (Usually a lot of laughter here.)

"Well . . ."

"And how much more might you be willing to pay if you thought you really had discovered the best babysitter in Ansley Park?"

"I'm not sure. I'm not sure I would still have found the best one. And again, Ashley is very, very good."

There is nothing unusual in this conversation. This is precisely how almost all choices of a service provider are made: you find someone you feel is very good, and you keep using them as long as they prove it.

The famous advertising man David Ogilvy once hinted at this when he bemoaned the same thing: the marketer's belief that they must position themselves as the Superior Choice, the very best of the best.

"Marketers waste too much time doing this," Ogilvy said. "You can get far more impact simply from convincing someone you are positively good."

And you can. Don't tell me you are the best; you are a salesperson, so I don't completely trust you anyway. Show me—with strong evidence—that you are positively good.

Again, that's what John Deere did to our tractor. For over a hundred years, they produced positively good products. Perhaps Simplicity was superior, but it didn't matter, and there was no way to prove it. The tractor buyers chose positively good.

Your biggest competitor is not a competitor. It's your prospect, and their reluctance to change, their suspicions of your motives, their fear of making a bad decision—of choosing the positively bad, all of which we will look into next.

But first: This isn't about being better. It's about being—in the mind of your prospect—positively good.

Overcoming "the Better Temptation"

For over 150 years, even the most experienced marketer believed the wisdom of the nineteenth-century American essayist Ralph Waldo Emerson. "Build a better mousetrap"—a product provably better than any existing one—"and the world will beat a path to your door."

In the 1960s, a communications scholar dressed up the "better mousetrap" idea to make it sound more scientific. He called it "relative advantage" and suggested what seems obvious: people prefer better things to merely good ones. So offer a service or product with some "relative advantage" the smart thinking went, and you will succeed.

Relying on this apparent perfect sense, American companies barraged us with new and improved products. But these better mousetraps didn't merely struggle. With few exceptions, they died young. And it wasn't just the you-must-be-kidding, *Saturday Night Live* parody products like Ben Gay Aspirin, Colgate Kitchen Entrees, and Frito Lay lemonade. It was almost everything.

Ninety-five percent of all new products, according to the Cincinnati research firm AcuPoll, failed.

What was going on?

In the June 2006 *Harvard Business Review,* a Harvard marketing professor and former Mobil oil executive, John Gourville, explained it in a compelling and cleverly named article, "Eager Sellers and Stony Buyers."

New products ask us to change, he reminded us. They ask us to change from one product to another. And as discussed in the section on Status Quo Bias, as much as we humans may like better, we hate change far more.

We are creatures of habit.

Gourville concluded that for "better" to work, a product cannot be merely much better than a current one. *It must be nine times better.* He had a famous ally: Intel's celebrated CEO Andy Grove, who said earlier that to be rapidly adopted, a new product had to offer benefits ten times greater than the current ones.

Unless your service is an order of magnitude better than your competitors, you need to stop thinking about selling "better." Better is vague; it is a mere matter of opinion—and no one trusts a marketer's claim of "better" anyway.

Instead, think about your current prospects' habits.

What are those habits?

Write them in a narrative.

Then write a narrative that shows you understand their reluctance and you have a solution that requires the least possible change in their current habits.

Forget "Better." Think "Help."

The Challenge: Talking to Yourself

A loving person lives in a loving world. A hostile person lives in a hostile world. Everyone you meet is your mirror."

Ken Keyes, a master in modern self-help techniques, put that perfectly: we think other people are just like us. Again, the psychologists have a term for this cognitive bias of ours; it's called "the False Consensus Effect."

The False Consensus Effect leads me to write and design messages that appeal to me, because I assume other people think and feel like I do. So they will find that message appealing, too.

But like you, I am not my prospects. What works on you and me often doesn't work on someone else.

How painfully I know this.

Some people thrive with company, for example. This means that an excellent way to attract those people as clients is to host a large event. And hallelujah, they come.

Unfortunately, the introverts don't.

We're all different.

Some want just the facts. Others want the full context. (Men tend toward the first, women to the second.)

Some are impressed by credentials. Others view them as chest-thumping.

Some people want to direct the meeting. Others want to be led.

Some feel passionately about what's in it for them. Others want to know what's in it for the people they care most about.

This is happening right now in this book. Some of you are rushing through these stories to each conclusion, while others are lingering and pondering.

This is enormously significant for your marketing. How do you make sure your messages will work? Specifically, how do you make sure they work on everyone other than the person you see in the mirror?

Ask colleagues and friends—at least five.

Show them your message, promise, and evidence. But don't ask what they think of it, because you might not get one suggestion. Ask instead, "What three things could I do to improve this?"

Asking for three things compliments each person. It tells them you think they have good ideas and critical eyes.

But always do this: make sure your message appeals to us, and not just you.

Persuade us, not you.

Themes

A longtime employee of a famous company, shaking her head at its recent history, confided she had crafted the perfect slogan for them.

"I'm going with, 'One hundred and twenty-five years of tradition unmarred by progress.'"

After a lifetime of seeing advertisements, it's easy for you to assume that you need a slogan, your very own "When It Absolutely Positively Has to Be There Overnight."

It's a good idea, but not for the reason you assume. Even the famous and memorable slogans left us long ago. The US Army's brilliant "Be All You Can Be" lived for only twenty years. One of its successors, "Army Strong," lived for just nine. Even great slogans have short shelf lives.

You don't need a slogan for us; you need one for you. Crafting the few best words that express your core promise to your prospects can help you focus the message you deliver face-to-face, as well as serve as your three-second elevator speech.

And there often is one more benefit: the "Little Engine That Could" Effect.

Positive self-talk works. Repeating "I can make a difference in people's lives," which is what every good service must do, increases the chance that you can and the conviction you demonstrate to prospects. That is what Arnold Munk, the Little Engine's creator, wanted to convey: not just hard work, but the importance of positive self-talk, just as the group Journey reminded everyone three times in their famous song: "Don't Stop Believin'."

Craft your theme, and repeat it often.

The Age of Faster

People today don't want speeches. They want sound bites.

They don't want the whole book. They want the article the book should have been.

They don't want the voice message that takes forty-five seconds to check and hear. They want the text message that takes five.

Years ago, they showed they didn't want the whole story. They wanted the summary, and *USA Today* answered them.

They don't want a one-hour lecture. They want it in twelve minutes, and TED answered them.

Make it short. Then make it shorter.

Robert Jensen's Perfect Advice

Four words was all it took.

The designer Robert Jensen briefly scanned a new client's website and said it only needed one change:

Fewer words, better words.

How to Be an Expert

You want to be seen as an expert, and we've seen that you can suggest this by positioning yourself as a specialist. Again, a veterinarian who specializes in cancer in dogs looks more expert than one who handles any and all potentially terminal canine diseases.

The next trait of an expert, however, matters even more and takes us to an excellent place to see how experts are judged: America's courthouses.

Every day in every major city, several experts will testify for one side, and several for the other, in a trial. And non-experts like you and me—jurors—will be asked to weigh their conflicting opinions and decide which expert they trust most.

What experts do jurors trust most?

Fortunately, we can look to experts on this subject. The consultants at DecisionQuest, in 10 offices nationwide, have over 30 years of experience consulting in all 50 states on over 18,000 high-risk engagements, and have studied the question and answered it with a story of a particular case.

The case involved expert testimony on geology. Side one retained a high school teacher with a master's degree in geology from a local university. Side two chose a Harvard graduate with years of experience working for a geological exploration company.

Which man seemed "more expert" to the jurors? The high school teacher. Why? The experts at DecisonQuest explained:

"Jurors focus on experience, while attorneys focus on credentials." And then DQ's critical conclusion:

"Jurors focus on a witness's ability to teach them."

An expert isn't someone with knowledge. An expert is someone who can teach what they know.

To be a better marketer, become a better teacher.

And What Makes a Better Teacher?

The mediocre teacher tells. The good teacher explains. The superior teacher demonstrates."

This quote from William Arthur Ward captures it: a great teacher—and therefore, the person your prospects will regard as an expert—knows a subject so well, they can explain it to anyone.

And how do teachers explain it, and how should you? The experts at DecisionQuest answer that question in a way that will not surprise readers of this book:

"Telling a story is the most persuasive way to communicate."

Stories demonstrate. Your stories take an abstract principle and make it concrete, in a story that makes your listener say, "I get it."

To be seen as an expert, learn to tell stories.

The Enemy Called the Adjective

The great French essayist Paul Valéry, twelve times nominated for the Nobel Prize, hated us copywriters. He'd written before mass advertising arrived, and died in 1945 as it was taking hold. And he loathed us for stealing from him—and all good writers—one of the eight parts of speech.

"Advertising," he wrote, "has annihilated the power of the most powerful adjectives."

We stole "unique," turned it into "most unique," then annihilated it with "truly the most unique." We went on to carpet-bomb every superlative we could spot. "Superior" died under the attack of "world-class," which left only "universe-class."

So, perhaps we ruined adjectives, but eventually we will improve marketing. If you can't use a mere adjective like "world-class," you have to replace it with something far more compelling: proof.

And you should.

Mark Twain offered the solution to Valéry's problem. "Three simple words on adjectives," he wrote. "Leave them out."

At a different point, Twain added the perfect conclusion to this:

"When in doubt, just tell the truth."

Adjectives, however, are mostly fat; they weaken the body and slow it down. "Dedicated staff," "cutting-edge solutions," "a proactive approach"—you already are drifting away. You've been there and read those. If the road to hell, as author Stephen King once said, "is paved with adverbs," the alternate route is littered with adjectives.

And marketing communications are littered with adjectives, too. Consider these famous repeat offenders—and strike them from everything you write:

> *Actionable, client-centric, collaborative, committed, cost-effective, creative, cutting-edge, devoted, experienced, high-level, holistic, industry-leading, innovative, leading-edge, mission-critical, next-generation, outside-the-box, outstanding, proactive, responsive, robust, scalable, seamless, state-of-the-art, superior, sustainable, synergistic, value-added*

These adjectives lead every marketer on the road to hell. They say nothing other than to hint you are writing on autopilot.

Don't tell us you are outstanding. Show us.

Don't tell us you are innovative. Show us.

Don't tell us you are committed, dedicated, or devoted. *Show us.*

More proof, fewer adjectives.

Empty Words

All of the following are taken verbatim from the first paragraph of well-known company websites.

"A tradition of excellence."

A question: What's in that for the reader?

"Celebrating 50 years of service."

Same question: What's in that for the reader?

"A leading international mid-market company serving . . . Helping our clients solve their toughest problems."

Your competitors solve only easy problems?

"The fifth largest . . . in the country."

Would larger be better for me? Would smaller? What makes you think that fifth is just right?

"A commitment to excellence."

As opposed to a commitment to what? Being less than excellent?
What are you saying?

You aren't saying anything. You are just filling up the "About Us" space on your website.

Stop writing and start telling us something. Tell us a story. Wrap a fact in an emotion that compels us to act.

Answer the question of every prospect: "How can you make my life just a little better?"

No clichés, no hollow promises.

Your Images

The Decline of the Word and the Rise of the Image

We live in a world where not needing your receipt for a salad at Whole Foods is an "awesome" decision.

It's a world where book covers insist that a hundred different events "changed America forever." It's a world where several internet headlines each day promise us something that "will change forever" what we think about some thing, such as cats, swimsuits, or Britney Spears, or that a comedian's graduation speech "will change your life forever."

It's a world where a book that sells ten thousand copies—the population of Sandy, the forty-seventh-largest town in Oregon—is called a "national bestseller."

It's a world with more than a dozen "*The* Feel Good" movies of the summer. We can expect that next year will bring a dozen Feel-Best movies of the summer, followed by a dozen Feel Best Movies That Changed Life Forever . . .

Linguists always have said that languages evolve, but ours seems to have devolved. It now seems in the clutches of a huge talking egg:

"'When I use a word,' Humpty Dumpty said, in rather a scornful tone, 'it means just what I choose it to mean—neither more nor less.'"

It's the Age of Word Hyperinflation. So, heaven help the business that promises its products are merely "highly regarded and very popular." Admit it: that rings as "not too bad at all," doesn't it?

When word after word loses its meaning, we learn to mistrust all of them. When those words come from marketers, we disregard them entirely. Which means something quite profound:

Words fail us now, literally.

Which means that we have to rely on something else instead:

Images.

The Sheer Force of Images

She loved the song.

Bob, Bob, Bob, Bob, Bob or Ann?

Bob or Ann, take my hand,

Bob or Ann!

Perhaps if you read that quickly, and have heard The Beach Boys' classic song "Barbara Ann," you recognize those three lines as a parody of that song.

But it's not. "Bob or Ann" is what a woman named Betsy heard whenever she heard the song.

Marketers spend weeks trying to craft a particular message. Months later, they learn that many people missed their point.

Or they didn't hear it. They saw it.

A vivid example: In 1985, we created a series of commercials for a bank. We wanted to convey how important that good information was to one's success in anything. We decided to demonstrate that point with unusual true stories of a local fencer, a composer, and a man planning an ascent of Mt. Everest, showing how each used information to succeed.

For the mountain climber spot, we showed the climber reading weather reports, studying the route of previous climbs, and comparing equipment options. Repeatedly, the commercial's voice-over talked about information and concluded by telling listeners that our client bank had the information "you need to succeed."

We previewed the commercials to focus groups. "What did the spot communicate to you?" we asked.

Perhaps one viewer in ten mentioned the word "information." What did most people hear?

"They're talking about *strength*. They're saying their bank is strong, solid."

Trying to hide our confusion, we asked, "What did the commercial say to give you that impression?"

"The mountain. It showed the man rock climbing there. The bank wants to look strong, like the mountain and the climber."

That had never occurred to us. We did not intend to suggest "strength." But our commercial did. The three-second clip of the climber scaling a rock wall overcame the repeated words of the announcer about the value of information.

Sometimes, people hear what we say. But with surprising frequency, they hear "Bob, Bob or Ann?" or see a rock climber for three seconds and hear "solid and strong."

It reminds one of the fallibility of eyewitnesses, where three witnesses give three irreconcilably different versions of what happened. Our belief in our own ability to see things accurately leads us to put faith in eyewitnesses—a faith that has eroded steadily in recent years as DNA testing has shown that hundreds of men convicted of crimes based on eyewitnesses "seeing them" could not have been at the site of the crime.

Despite our self-confidence in everything concerned with our brains, including our perception, we are not keen-eyed observers or flawless listeners. That's partly because our minds often are pondering several things at once—watching a commercial while thinking about work, for example.

And it reminds us that, sometimes, a picture outshouts a hundred words. *We think with our eyes.*

Which means you should be as careful about what you show as you are about what you say.

Today, the visual overwhelms the verbal.

The Kings of Orange

Every twenty-five seconds, someone somewhere in the world buys a Hermes scarf.

No fair-minded marketer would argue that this occurs primarily only because of the Hermes brand. Hermes scarves are made fanatically, from over seven thousand color combinations, each scarf individually silk-screened on the world's finest Chinese silk.

And perhaps Hermes's ingenious founder, Thierry Hermes, was not a branding genius. Maybe he merely liked the color that would one day be the unmistakable Hermes orange, a color second in brand identifiability only to Tiffany's signature robin's-egg blue.

These famous orange bags helped imprint the Hermes name in people's minds; they boosted Hermes's "I've-heard-of-you-ness."

Choose a distinctive color and deploy it relentlessly.

The Copycat Kings of Orange

For our next story, we leave Hermes's headquarters on Rue de Foubourg Saint-Honoré, grab a taxi, and direct it south southwest exactly fifteen minutes to the headquarters of a company that copied Hermes—and then went one step further.

We have arrived at—literally—Orange.

Aware of the power of the Hermes orange, the marketers who came up with the name Orange—a huge telecommunications company now in mobile, landline, and internet—took the orange color a dramatic step further. They tied their name to the color and then amplified the combined effect by tying their tagline to both. The result—the memorable "The Future's Bright, the Future's Orange"—is among the most successful in marketing history. (For a comparable American example, consider UPS's 2002–2010 "What can brown do for you?" campaign.)

Orange's new line gave Orange perhaps the greatest "I've-heard-of-you-ness" in all of Europe. "The Future's Orange" message was so compelling that the company continued to use it for fourteen years—an eternity in twenty-first-century marketing.

Deliver your messages in a distinctive colored package.

The Age of the Eye

Not long ago, major buildings were rectangular, shirts were white and ties were black, and newspapers were both—but only both and no other color.

Then along came Frank Gehry to make buildings that resembled explosions, Giorgio Armani and Ralph Lauren to make men care about pleats and Sea Island cotton, and *USA Today* to splash out a newspaper in the colors of Fisher-Price toys.

We grew up reading letters and memos in one of two styles: Pica and Elite. Now, Microsoft offers forty-nine different typefaces just in fonts with names beginning with "C."

Our television pictures once were fuzzy, then no-def, then mid-def. Now we own iPads with Retina displays and soon will be able to watch televisions with 8K resolution—twice beyond what our eyes can appreciate.

Words continue to fail us—we've read *Why Johnny Can't Read* and *Why Johnny Can't Write* for decades—so we have rushed in images to fill the void. And we should. A recent study found that readers spend just 5.6 seconds on the copy in the average website—*and 6.5 seconds on the primary image.*

Read that again, and remember it.

Aware that we are becoming more a nation of lookers than readers, designers have flooded the web with infographics, confident that a graphic will deliver better "info" than any words can.

Our grandparents lived in a world where you could own any color of car you chose, as long as you chose black. And for years, computers reflected a similar belief. They were machine gray to suggest that computers were merely machines. Steve Jobs decided otherwise and introduced iMacs in grape, tangerine, lime, and orange. He knew that, in this new world, covers matter as much as the books they cover.

You once could own any kind of Levis you wanted, as long as they were blue denim 501s that were three inches too long. Today, you can buy Levis in 501, 504, 505, 510, 511, 513, 514, 517, 522, 527, 550, 555, 560, and 569, and at least thirty-five different colors and finishes, including Barbary, black, and three different stonewashes, plus rinse, rigid, and rugged, not to mention kale, white bull, and ice cap.

In the Age of the Eye, we no longer need to watch a mere football game. At AT&T Stadium in Dallas, we can watch the game on the stadium's 550-ton, 1,080 pixel–resolution video screen that stretches from one 20-yard line to the opposite one, illuminated with 30 million light bulbs. If that screen isn't big enough, we can switch allegiances and cheer the Jacksonville Jaguars whose video screen and scoreboard is 60 feet wider than their football field is long.

It's the Age of the Eye, where images matter and pictures tell several thousand words. And you must enter it.

What do your images do to advance your business?

Is It Your Book, Or Your Cover?

No one buys pale oranges. Why would you? You only want the most delicious.

But the orangeness of a peel means nothing. Oranges are picked when they are pale, usually with significant yellow green in their skin. Workers then spray them with ethylene gas to turn them orange. The orangeness is a trick; the cover has been dressed up. The book is the same.

And the trick works. You choose the orangest orange. Even now that you know it is a trick—that the orangeness of the peel has nothing to do with the juiciness of the orange—you still will choose the orangest oranges. I'm told that we are foolish to choose the orangest oranges, but I choose them, too.

That's the power of packages, including yours. They fool us for better, as in the case of the orange, even when we know better.

Look carefully at your peel. The context changes the content.

The Power of the Image

Item One:

Andrew Stevniak dreamed of parlaying his intense 285 pounds into a college football scholarship. Suspecting that his presentation style might affect the college coaches who were recruiting him, a group of researchers helped Andrew present his case in three different forms.

The first presented his statistics on a white sheet of paper.

The second presented them in bar graphs.

The third, a colorful PowerPoint presentation, put them in animated bar graphs that grew and shrank.

So how good of a football scholarship candidate was young Andrew? Well, that depended.

One Seemingly Tiny Change

In 1995, Coors launched Blue Moon beer. The Belgian-style wheat beer won over fans at Colorado Rockies games but not many others. The surge started months later, when Coors' salespeople persuaded bartenders to serve the beer with a wedge of orange. By 2008, Blue Moon was America's largest-selling craft beer.

In 2008, Interstate Bakeries filed for bankruptcy protection. One year later, they announced a 7 percent revenue increase. What had changed? They had updated the packaging for their iconic Twinkies, Ho Hos, and Ding Dongs.

In 2008, Seagram's wine coolers weren't selling. By mid-2009, they had captured 36 percent of the wine cooler market. What changed? The packaging—Seagram's repackaged the wine coolers in beer-like bottles.

In the midst of these three events, an executive named Bonnie Engler invited me to her offices at Pilgrim Cleaners, which operated nineteen locations in the Twin Cities. "Thank you for your books," she said. "They convinced me to change our signage." (I politely did not mention that her previous Olde English logo looked like it might read, "Ebenezer Scrooge," and that her old signs made it appear that her cleaners actually might cater only to Pilgrims.)

"Has there been an impact?" I asked.

"Oh my," Bonnie answered. "Our revenues are up well over 20 percent."

"Did you make other changes that might have contributed to this?"

"Nothing. Just those new signs."

In today's rush of time and crush of competitors, your name and logo often are all we know of you. Your logo acts as your suit, shoes, briefcase, and service vehicle. How does yours look?

How *should* it look?

Details matter—especially for your signature look.

Your Symbol

Don't give me some symbol for our company," the executive insists. "We aren't like a soft drink. We have a story. Just tell it."

The executive misunderstands. He tells his company's story with words, but words are merely symbols, too. The word "hat" is not a hat, after all. It's simply a symbol for a hat, composed of three letters.

And most images are more vivid than words. We react far more strongly to an American flag than to the words "American flag," just as the Nazi flag provokes far more controversy than the word "Nazi."

And one more thing: It is relatively easy to create a distinctive visual image, but nearly impossible to create a unique word. If you are able to do that, it's likely that no one will understand it.

We tell stories with nothing more than symbols. And visual images are the simplest, fastest, and most memorable way to communicate. They are pictures, after all. And, in the words of homespun wisdom, are truly worth a thousand words.

Your visuals are worth a thousand words.

Capitalizing on Halo Effects

Edward Thorndike became suspicious. The well-known psychologist detected an odd correlation between a soldier's physique and their commanding officer's impressions of that soldier.

Are soldiers with thick chests and arms and trim waists smarter? You'd think not. Are soldiers with those physiques more effective leaders? More reliable, honest, and courageous?

Again, you'd think not.

But commanding officers in Thorndike's studies disagree with you. They rated soldiers with excellent physiques to be smarter, more effective, more reliable, and more honest than soldiers with less impressive frames. Thorndike famously labeled this the Halo Effect, and it's been confirmed in dozens of studies since.

In 1974, sixty male undergraduate students were asked to rate three essays. One was deliberately well written, the second was poorly written, and the third was neither good nor bad. The students were given one of the first two essays along with one of two photographs meant to represent the authors—either one of an attractive women or one of a woman made to appear unattractive. The third essay was not accompanied by an author photo.

The students gave the attractive author's well-written essay an average score of 6.7. The same essay written by the unattractive author? A 5.9. And the unattractive writer was penalized even more for the poorly written essay. Students gave the attractive author a 5.1 for that "essay"—and the unattractive author a 2.7.

I began noticing the same effect in 1988. I heard this for the first time then and often over the next twenty-five years from venture capitalists: "It's a great business concept, but we'll need another CEO to run it."

This CEO wasn't experienced? He was. He lacked the education and training? Not at all. Then he lacked the basic skills needed for the role? No.

What made him unqualified then?

"He doesn't look the part," the VC would tell me. "He doesn't have CEO presence."

But wait, this is America. Anyone can grow up to be president, but only a few people can become a CEO? Really? And why?

"He doesn't look the part."

We judge books by their covers and people, and the businesses they run, by their appearance. We operate on Halo Effects.

And we live by the reverse as well, as those imagined "unattractive authors" discovered. These are known as Horns Effects. A good package prompts your prospects to conclude you are adept at what you do. A bad one has a Horns Effect.

But, in our defense, what choices do we have in judging the person providing a service? How do we decide the accountant filed a "good return" for us? If we understand enough about accounting to make that assessment, we could have done the return by ourselves.

How do we know if you give good legal advice or sound therapeutic recommendations? That your fillings are somehow better than the dentist in our nearest suburb? That you can plan my future better than the guy with that very impressive website and the nice accompanying photograph?

It's not that we're shallow. It's that we have little to go on but appearances, and appearances affect us.

Give yourself the handsomest possible halo.

The Power of Your Signature

When you think of the great brands, what images come to mind?

You think of their signatures: you see the Golden Arches, Shell's shell, Target's target, and Nike's swoosh.

These signatures help imprint each brand in your mind. They make the brands memorable.

Now consider some famous people who also are brands.

Andy Warhol had that amazing shock of white hair. And so do Virgin's Richard Branson with his lion's mane and Nike's Phil Knight and his platinum Afro. They're signatures.

Albert Einstein had that mad scientist's hair, too, along with the gray suits. He owned four identical ones.

Which brings us logically to the Man in Black (Johnny Cash) and the Man in White (author Tom Wolfe in his signature all-white summer suits).

David Letterman's signature was subtle, but hard to miss. It wasn't his dark suits in fabrics from London's Savile Row and cut with a suppressed waist, although those dark suits set off the contrast.

It was his almost-white socks.

Steve Jobs might have had the signature to end them all. Every day, he wore the same black St. Croix mock turtleneck (he owned a dozen at a time), same blue Levis 501 straight-leg jeans, and same white New Balance 991 sneakers. ("I don't like friction," he said. "Having to think about what to put on each morning creates too much friction.")

Your name can be your signature, too. That was the insight that created Faith Popcorn and Lady Gaga, and that inspired Earl Woods when he decided to name his child Tiger.

The job of every good marketer is to help make his clients' brands stick in people's minds. So we try to create one-of-a-kind names and logos.

Find a signature.

Don't Just Write It. Sign It.

You know it's *Time* magazine from the signature red frame around the cover image.

Just as you know *National Geographic* from its nearly identical gold frame.

And you know it's *Vanity Fair.* You know from its typeface (a proprietary font known as Didot) and from the obsessively staged cover shots by the legendary Annie Leibovitz.

These are the repeating devices these three publications use to ensure that when we read their magazine, we know and remember it was *Time*, "NatGeo" (a signal that they chose too long a name), and *Vanity Fair*.

You should do this with your content, too. Make sure everything you print, publish, and distribute bears your distinctive stamp.

Ideally, find and repeat a distinctive color. That's a favorite device of Hermes (burnt orange, Pantone 16-1448 TPX), Tiffany (a light robin's-egg blue protected by trademark and privately registered with Pantone as PMS 1837, the number representing the year Tiffany was founded), and Twitter (Pantone 298 blue). And of Yahoo! (Pantone Violet C) and Starbucks (Pantone 3425 C).

Because your service is personal, include a photo and use the same one repeatedly. And place it in the same position on your material.

You should title your entire series of articles. Unless there is a compelling reason not to, include either your or your business's name in the title. Think Beckwith on Brands, Tiger's Tips, and Leibovitz on Lighting.

You want to do everything you can to build familiarity with your name. And you never want a reader to tell a friend, "I read this excellent series on (your topic here)," without being able to identify the author.

Make everything you publish look like yours, and only yours.

A Tiny Tweak That Can Change Everything

Years ago, an ambitious young family law attorney peeked into my open office door in Minneapolis's Lumber Exchange Building.

"I wonder if you could help me," he asked.

I said perhaps I could.

Like many family practitioners in those old days, Doug was running a small Yellow Pages ad. His ads were almost working; Doug was getting fourteen calls a month.

I thought I could improve the ad. And with just two tweaks, I did.

We sent the new ad to the company. Early one morning, four weeks after the ad first appeared, I turned to see Doug peeking into my office door again. He was smiling. Our ad was performing almost too well. He'd had to hire a temp to screen his flood of calls and set up interviews.

Yet I'd made only two changes.

I'd changed the headline to read "For You. And for Your Kids." And I'd added a black-and-white photo of Doug.

As I've said, pictures tell a thousand words, and a black-and-white photo of a kind-looking and attractive family law attorney prompted forty more people every month to call Doug.

As with the old yellow media, so it is with our new. Ask any social media expert how to boost responses to a blog or a tweet—Twitter's most recent data shows that tweets with pictures were retweeted 35 percent more often than text-only tweets—and one of their first suggestions will be the tip I gave Doug decades ago:

Add a photograph.

We are drawn to images. They appeal to us in ways words cannot.

And as this book stresses repeatedly, your service is not an enterprise. People don't buy a haircut or help with a tax return; they buy the person providing that service. So your marketing needs to show you immediately. *You are the service.*

Use pictures everywhere you can.

P.S. This story ends very happily, by the way. Twenty-two years later, I was grocery shopping in St. Paul and felt a tap on my shoulder. It was Doug, still remarkably young-looking, and his familiar, warm smile told me he had more good news to share.

"I've retired," he said. "And I want to thank you. That ad was what started it all."

"But Packaging Is Just Gift Wrap"

You may think all that matters is the quality of your service and whatever message you persuasively communicate. Anything else is mere packaging.

This comes very close to how analyticals view marketing. Build a better mousetrap and explain it. Intelligent people will buy it.

But you can convince even an ultra-analytic that this conclusion is wrong with this test.

Take a swatch of yellow paper and put it on a background of white.

Look at the yellow paper.

Now pull out the white sheet and replace it with a black one.

Now look at the yellow paper.

It's a radically different yellow. The yellow on plain white looked soft and washed-out. But it leapt off the black background. The difference almost blinded you. The difference also explains why traffic signs sport black symbols against yellow backgrounds: it's the world's most visible contrast. (It's why the original cabs were painted yellow and black, too. It was to ensure that no one, including other drivers, could miss them or hit them.)

The context changed your entire perception of the yellow: even though it was *the exact same piece of yellow.*

An audience for a speech will hear three different speeches from the same speaker if she dresses more casually than her audience for the first, just a little dressier than them for the second, and much dressier for the third. The second speech will sound the best—the most informed, the most helpful, and the most interesting.

The context changed their perception of the content.

Repeated studies show that women find men in red more attractive, and vice versa. (That may explain why both Chris de Burgh's and Lorrie Morgan's songs about women in red became hits, and the Gene Wilder movie about a man's obsession with a woman was *The Woman in Red.* We understood the attraction; we got the singers' message.)

I loved Susan's Casey's book *The Wave*, about the world's biggest waves—which are falling wet cliffs, really—and the borderline lunatics who try to ride down them. I was about to rave about her book on Amazon when I noticed its score for low reviews. I decided to read some.

They were harsh.

I guess the reviews influenced me because I no longer loved the book as much as I thought I did. I left without doing what I had come there to do: post a five-star review.

The context—seeing that book against this new background—changed the content.

This is another reminder that everything about you and your service matters in your marketing. It's the context for your content.

Improve any part of your context and you improve the content.

Fixing one part of your service fixes several.

And your packaging really *matters in the fix.*

How to Think Like a Designer

You probably are not a designer. But eventually, and more often than once, you will have to assess something designed for your business: your card, your website, your space.

You might begin with the old conviction "Beauty is in the eye of the beholder," from which you decide that design is about beauty and that anyone's opinion is only that: mere opinion.

But design involves more than simple aesthetics. Ultimately, your design should please almost everyone's eye and displease no one's. Beyond that, however, your design should cast a nice reflection on you, and quickly.

These are the first four design rules I ask from clients. I urge you to have these rules alongside you each time you make a design-related decision.

Is it beautiful?
Do your five closest friends honestly agree?

Is it clear?

If more than one person asks, "What does this mean?" keep working.

Is it simple?

If there's clutter, a prospect might see only the clutter and miss your message. Just as good writing employs only as many words as it needs to convey its message, and not a word more, good design includes only what it absolutely needs.

Is it honest?

Good design, like a good person, never makes a promise it cannot keep. Don't make yourself something you are not. The world will figure that out and never trust you again.

First four principles: make it beautiful, clear, simple, and honest.

The First Rule of Images

Living in the major hub of two big American corporations, Target and Delta Air Lines, proved to be perfect for this test. I asked twenty Minnesotans to draw and describe the Target logo. Nineteen said, "It's a target." (The twentieth person thought it was a circle.)

Sixteen could draw it perfectly: a large bull's-eye surrounded by one white and one red ring.

I then asked them to draw and describe the logo for Delta Air Lines, an airline for which nine of them were registered frequent fliers.

A man who had migrated to Minnesota from Greece said it was the Greek letter Delta, but drew the logo as a simple triangle, which it isn't.

An engineer said, "It's the symbol for change, which is Delta." No one else could name or draw Delta's logo. It literally was Greek to them. (I studied Greek for two years and never made the connection between the airline's name, Delta, and its Greek delta symbol.)

Almost everything you need to know about using images in your marketing—including for your logo—can be deduced from this exercise.

The First Rule of Images, One More Time: Pictures beat words.

There's a good reason no one has ever complained to you, "I have a terrible time with faces, but I never forget a name." We simply remember images of things better than a collection of letters from the alphabet.

Dozens of studies have shown this. It's called the Picture Superiority Effect. If someone shows you a photo of a Labradoodle, you are six times more likely to remember it than you would be to remember a picture of the word "dog."

You easily can understand why. Pictures are filled with details. They are what experts call "perceptually rich." A photo of a dog shows colors, contrasts, the dog's expression, a sense of the texture of the dog's fur and the grass under its feet.

A photo of the word "dog," however, shows you nothing more than three commonplace characters from the twenty-six in our alphabet. Letters are almost perceptually broke.

And our mind easily can confuse letters when letters are all we see. Three days from now, you will have trouble remembering whether I am now showing you the word "quilt" rather than the word "guilt." Those two words look almost indistinguishable yet describe two things that are less alike than the words "octopus" and "Adele."

But not all pictures are more memorable than words. This leads us to . . .

The Second Rule of Images

The Second Rule of Images: If people cannot label your image, they will not remember it.

Minnesotans remember the Target logo because it gives them two ways to remember it: as a word, "Target," and as an image, "a target."

Psychologists refer to this as Paivio's Dual-Coding Theory. Our brains employ two codes for pictures: the image itself, and the word we use to describe the image. If our brain can code the image twice—as a word and as an image—we are far more apt to remember it.

This explains why Minnesotans cannot remember the Delta logo—unless they are from Greece or practice as engineers. They don't have a word for it. It might as well just be the word "Delta."

Choose images people can label.

The Third Rule of Images

The Third Rule of Images: People remember distinctive images dramatically better than common ones.

The Delta symbol is basically a triangle. How many companies use triangles in their logo? Just for starters: Adobe, Adidas, AOL, Bass Ale, Citgo, Guess, Marlboro, Mitsubishi, Toblerone, and Valvoline. Add the dozens of enterprises in your area that represent themselves—or try to—with a triangle, and you might wonder: *Why did they bother creating a logo at all?*

This also helps explain why you must avoid stock photos. These images literally are "stock": people have seen them, or too-close variations of them, too many times. These images have become so familiar that we have no reason to look at them, much less process whatever information they are meant to convey. These images say nothing new, yet your images represent your best opportunity for saying something that people will notice and remember.

Again, people spend more time looking at the images on your website than on the words. (And more time looking at your logo, too.) These images are critical content.

So, what are your images saying?

Do they have the characteristics that will make them stick in people's minds?

If you've been featured or quoted in a publication, don't tell your readers. Show them an image of the publication's cover.

If you've won an award, show the trophy.

If you have served a well-known client, show their logo.

If you've helped someone lose fifteen pounds or created their new sun deck, show us the before and after.

Whatever you do, show more and tell less.

Show works many times better than tell.

Persuasion's Strangest Force

In the spring of 1983, a couple was savoring their after-dinner coffee at New Orleans's famous restaurant Arnaud's when a man approached them.

"How is your coffee?" he asked.

The woman said, "Rich." Her companion said, "Delightful."

———

In 2006, Harvard professor Ellen Langer told a group of hotel workers that their housekeeping work was good exercise and "met the guidelines for a healthy and active lifestyle." Over the next month, those workers lost an average of two pounds and enjoyed a 10 percent drop in their systolic blood pressure.

———

In 2009, an interviewer approached fifty diners who had been invited to the New York restaurant Tuscani to sample the chef's new pasta dishes.

The diners called the dishes "great" and "excellent," and one said, "perfect!"

————

Throughout the last two decades, women and men in different parts of America were given New Extra Strength Rogaine. After twenty-one days, 40 percent reported new hair growth.

————

Each of these stories, however, ends in a catch.

The "fabulous" coffee at Arnaud's that night did not come from a French press. It came from a jar of Folgers freeze-dried crystals. The diners' responses were captured in a famous series of hidden-camera commercials.

A second group of Boston hotel workers who were not told their work was good exercise showed no change in weight, body fat percentage, or blood pressure.

Tuscani's chef had not prepared the pasta dishes; Pizza Hut had. They were its new Tuscani pastas, snuck into the Italian restaurant to see if New York foodies could tell the difference. Their responses also were captured by thirty hidden cameras and shown in a Pizza Hut Tuscani pasta commercial.

And those Rogaine users who spotted new hair? Minoxidil, the active ingredient in hair restoration products like Rogaine, does promote hair growth in many people. But those users were not given minoxidil. If the vegetable oil in their control substance actually promoted hair growth, bald people could cure themselves with tossed salads.

But they can't, and don't.

What is at work in these cases? Placebo Effects. (Worth adding: People exposed to fake poison ivy develop real rashes.)

The lesson is that we experience what we expect to. If we taste coffee or pasta in an outstanding restaurant, or sample a product we think grows hair, or we perform work that we believe is good exercise, our expectations change the outcomes. In fact, it's accurate to say this:

Our expectations become the outcomes.

This has enormous meaning to marketers. Your marketing does more than draw people to your business; it influences their experiences. If your marketing primes them to believe their experience will be good, they are more likely to have good experiences.

But you've been exposed to this more than once. Every speech you've ever heard probably was primed. The introducer assured you the speaker can jump higher, dive in deeper, and come out drier than anyone. She knows that mere promise increases the likelihood you will end up feeling informed, entertained, and inspired.

And you are. So:

To improve your clients' experience, improve the messages you deliver before you deliver the service.

Your Marketing Changes the Experience

The primary purpose of your marketing is to produce clients.

But there's another purpose that may never have occurred to you. It didn't occur to me until I studied it:

It's to lead your clients to love your service.

Your marketing does not merely coax prospects to choose you. It sets their expectations of your service. If people expect your service to be wonderful, they are more apt to think it is.

It's because we experience what we expect to—our expectations color every experience. Nothing demonstrates this more spectacularly than the Startling Case of the Six-Inch Nail.

Just after New Year's Day 2010, a twenty-nine-year-old British builder jumped from a landing and onto a six-inch nail with such force that the nail penetrated his boot and nearly came out the top. Seeing his extreme pain, his coworkers called emergency, and a car rushed the man to emergency.

The ER doctors found that barely touching the nail made the man scream, and they quickly sedated him. The young man suffered so much pain that the doctors administered fentanyl, a painkiller one hundred times more powerful than morphine.

With the patient sedated and the pain controlled, the doctors gently removed his work boot, and discovered something startling.

The nail had passed cleanly between the builder's toes. There was no injury at all.

What happened here? An example of the Nocebo Effect, one of the more bizarre examples of how our expectations change our perceptions and feelings. If we think we have a nail in our foot, it can hurt so much we need a near-lethal drug to reduce the agony.

Repeatedly, we see it: *what we expect changes what we feel.*

Your clients will tend to experience whatever they expect. Your marketing sets that expectation. The better your marketing is—the more polished, professional, and smart—the better the client's experience.

What does your business card lead me to expect?

What does your office lead me to expect?

Your jacket, your watch, your website—what do they lead me to expect?

Do they all make me expect an exceptional service from an exceptionally accomplished person?

Make us expect something exceptional, and it's more likely we will experience just that.

Be Like the Great Artists—Steal

You likely have heard that the genius of an artist is the ability to hide his sources. The artist doesn't truly steal but draws on everything that has come before him.

Fortunately for every marketer, it's easy to steal the best ideas and apply them. And the first robbery you should pull is from the most effective advertising of our lifetimes: Nike's.

Nike sells the hardest-to-sell commodity in the world: shoes. It's hard to do much with a shoe, after all. Add bells and whistles to one and you defeat a major purpose: the lightest possible weight and the maximum possible comfort.

Before you explore the details, look at the biggest possible picture. What does Nike advertise?

You naturally answer shoes. Nike doesn't advertise shoes. Entire Nike commercials never show shoes. You might reconsider and say athletic products. It doesn't sell those, either—at least if you go by the ads.

What does Nike sell?

It sells you.

It sells your desire to lead a more active and healthier life—to move, take up that sport, train for that 10K. It sells great athletes and great athletics, and your desire to live in that spirit but on a different scale.

This is what your marketing, beginning with your website, should sell: us. It should sell us on what we might experience if we decided to work with you.

Study Nike. Every single part.

Your Second Target: Apple

Arguably, Nike isn't the most successful advertiser in the world. If they are not, Apple is.

So just take forty-five seconds to steal from Apple's best thinking. Go to Apple's website. Then click on each of the items on the (bar) Mac. iPad. Watch. Phone. Music.

What is all that you see on each screen?

A single, beautifully photographed image, and a single, succinct headline. At this writing, the headlines are:

Light. Years Ahead.
Everything Changes on iPad.
The Watch Is Here.
Shot on iPhone 13.
Free Three-Month Trial of Apple Music.

Five panels, five images, twenty-two words.

Why does Apple say so little? Because in the digital age, you must. We don't have time. If your website immediately says, "I am going to steal lots of your time," we say, "No you aren't. Goodbye."

This isn't to argue you must be this succinct. Visitors to Apple's site know more about Apple than visitors to your site will know about you; most know almost nothing. But Apple's site is what people think of as quality, and it exemplifies after years of testing what works in web communication. You want to be associated with quality, of course, and you don't want to spend years of testing to see what works for your website. Don't. Reverse engineer Apple's site, figure out the obvious thinking behind it, and see how closely you can approximate it in your site.

How can you rely on one image and five words to move the prospect in your direction?

How can you be simpler?

Copy Apple. Because, after all, who could better understand this digital age, and how to market successfully in it, than the company that led us into it?

Study Apple.

The Meeting

Once again, we come to another moment that distinguishes marketing a product from marketing a service.

Carefully considered products, such as cars, high-end electronics, and medical devices, depend on expert salespeople. But most products—those you buy in retail stores and replace regularly—are merely marketed, and never sold.

Almost every service, by contrast, is both marketed and sold. No one plucks a consultant, a dentist, or a wedding photographer from a shelf. The marketing for services doesn't produce an immediate sale. It only prompts an inquiry, which may lead to the key event: the meeting.

In services, great marketing without a great meeting is the equivalent of a jet without engines: it looks terrific but it'll never fly.

So a book on marketing a service must talk about that key moment, the meeting.

To master marketing, master the meeting.

The Challenge: The Know-It-All Prospect

Not many years ago, all we knew of a business was what we read in its ads and brochures.

Now, we can find everything at the push of a button: Google's search button.

Thanks to Google, today's prospect owns an Encyclopedia Britannica of Businesses. Prospects for a personal trainer, for example, can quickly learn the pros and cons of protein-loading and the ten best ab exercises.

Today's prospect is an expert, too. I meet, for example, at least one nutrition expert every month. She tells me about the perils of gluten, the transformative power of kale, and the properties of every life-threatening ingredient in a can of chicken noodle soup.

Is nutrition her profession? Heavens no. She's a labor lawyer, a wealth manager, or a vice president of a credit union.

Clients for financial advice now know about basis points, for example, and have read that investing in an index mutual fund makes more sense than building a portfolio of stocks.

These clients know everything because they can: It's at their fingertips. For free.

That's your prospect, too. She has done her due diligence. She knows who you are, who you serve, and what you have accomplished. She may even know things that are not true; two of my prospects, for example, thought I ran a side business selling guns in Ocala, Florida.

What does this mean?

It means as a salesperson, you no longer pitch. You catch. Your well-informed prospect arrives at your first meeting and throws out several questions.

The best catcher wins.

Rehearse for the questions you expect. Practice the answers several times.

When Should You Meet with a Prospect?

How do your prospects decide?

Let's focus on one critical part: When do they decide—specifically, at what time of the day are they most receptive to your message?

Instinctively, you know not to call on Monday mornings. Too many prospects are unhappy to be there. And, knowing that prospects are already thinking about the weekend on Fridays, you probably know enough to avoid calling on those days.

But what is the best time to call? ("Is there a best time?" you may be asking. Yes.)

To answer this, consider the case of someone who makes her living making decisions: a judge.

Now give her a common decision such as a parole board decision. The judge will make up to thirty-five simple "yes" or "no" decisions each day. She either grants the prisoner's petition or refuses it.

Well, guess what's the most important influence on the judge's decision? When this was tested in courts in Israel, the answer was "breakfast and lunch."

At the start of each morning, judges grant about 65 percent of prisoners' requests. That quickly increases to almost 75 percent, then begins a staggered fall all the way to zero—yes, zero—just before the judge's lunch break.

What happens right after lunch? The prisoners apparently become far more deserving of parole: the judges grant parole to seven in ten. After that, they get tougher. The percentage of petitions they grant steadily declines to 12 percent—less than one in eight.

And what happens next? Judges take their afternoon meal break. When they return, they grant parole to almost two in three applicants. And then—yes—the percentage drops precipitously once more. At the end of the day, the tired judges grant parole to almost no one.

There's a saying familiar to lawyers: "Justice is what the judge had for breakfast." Perhaps we need to add "and lunch." But satisfied people are more receptive to our messages, and hungry people rarely are.

Good salespeople realize this without always knowing it. They book prospects for breakfasts and lunch, and make their sales pitches after their forks are down, and never before.

When's the best time to ask for someone's business? When they are satisfied—and when they are sated.

Time your sales calls: 9 AM and 1 PM.

The Most Effective Venue

When is the best time to meet a prospect?

It's breakfast, by several laps.

The reason is inherent in the very nature of what you are selling. A service is delivered eye-to-eye, face-to-face, and heart-to-heart. It necessarily follows that the best way to market a service is the same.

It's eye-to-eye, face-to-face. A prospect needs to look you in the eye, hear you speak, and listen to how you listen before deciding to have a relationship with you.

A website doesn't accomplish that. Nor does a banner ad, a tweet, or any other medium. (You might argue that "medium" describes these perfectly, because that describes their relative impact: medium at best.)

An experienced speaker will tell you why dinners don't work. A speaker learns to avoid dinner speeches; the audience is exhausted from their day. They don't want to be listening. They don't want to be doing anything but watching their current favorite streaming series or *Monday Night Football,* and perhaps not even that. Dinner needs to be after the end of a business day, and not part of it.

Plus, asking a new prospect for dinner sounds presumptuous. That's why smart people on dating sites know not to propose a first meeting at dinner. It's moving too fast. In the words of The Supremes' song, "You can't hurry love."

Lunches work, but less well. You know why from experience. At lunch, you still are thinking about a challenge from your morning, or one you will face that afternoon—or both.

Breakfasts work because they come at the beginning of a new day. We're rested. We're still full of hope. After our first sips of coffee, we can be downright jovial.

Book more breakfasts.

Prime the Meeting

Again, remember the sheer power of expectations for meetings, too. A client who expects a good meeting is more apt to experience one.

So prime the prospect. Send the prospect the most flattering possible resume of each of your people attending the meeting.

Impress them before you see them.

Pull

Great salespeople don't push. They pull.

They draw you in.

Pull, don't push.

"But Selling Is Slick"

I'm not a salesperson, and I don't want to be. I'm not slick or cocky, and I don't like shaking hands."

It's easy to dislike the very idea of selling. You have been conditioned to do so from childhood, from the ultimate con man, the Wizard of Oz, to stories of snake oil salesmen and movies like *Glengarry Glen Ross, Boiler Room,* and *The Wolf of Wall Street.* Selling is dishonest, salespeople are slick, and only the sleazy survive.

Before we look into those objections, it helps to consider this: living is selling. You prove it almost every day.

You started young. You coaxed your parents to take you to Disney World, raise your allowance, extend your curfew, and let you splurge on the prom. You pitched them on sleepovers, your first bike, and perhaps your first car. You sold them about that little slip in your grades and that little dent in Mom's car.

You kept selling. You probably sold a college on accepting you, an employer on hiring you, and your friends on going to your favorite restaurant.

You made each sale without reservation. You believed. And you proved you can sell whatever you believe in. You are halfway there.

But again, you insist you're not slick, not cocky, not a glad-hander. You're just not the salesperson type.

So let's address those objections.

"They're slick."

This is the stereotype of bad salespeople, but not the characteristic of great ones.

Great salespeople don't sell bills of goods. They passionately believe in their product and the company behind it.

"Only 10 percent of selling is persuasion," Shiv Khera has said. "Ninety percent is conviction."

"They're full of themselves."

They're not. None are bashful, but the best tend toward humility. It draws us to them. Great salespeople are like the athletes who win the Most Valuable Player trophies and tell the reporters, with obvious sincerity, "My team won this."

"They're glad-handers, backslappers, and the kind of people who are the life of the party."
Great salespeople are listeners, not talkers. This helps them understand us and our needs, a key to making every sale. Plus, great salespeople must listen, because one of our greatest wishes is simply to be listened to.

"They're competitive and aggressive."
Yes, they are. But that isn't selling.

So, life is a sale, and you are an experienced and proven salesperson already. The question is, how successful can you be?
Do you strongly believe in what you are offering?
Then you are 90 percent of the way there.
You have to sell anyway—and it's four-fifths believing.
P.S. Steve W. Martin, a professor of sales strategy at USC Marshall School of Business, performed personality tests on over one thousand salespeople and identified the top performers among them based on their memberships in the President's Club and annual performance. His research, reported in the June 27, 2011, Harvard Business Review in the article "Seven Personality Traits of Top Salespeople," supports each conclusion above.

Confidence

A service prospect wants assurance. He wants to feel free of those emotions that plague every prospect for a service: fear and doubt. He wants to feel confident that you will deliver.

The clues every prospect looks for, often without realizing it, are in you. Your confidence is a clue.

It's not bravado, boastfulness, or a bold handshake. It's actually quite different: it's the utter calm of the person without fear, the one who knows he can do it.

Confidence is a force multiplier.

Your Clients Are Mostly Geniuses

This isn't meant as a joke about men's egos. The dating website iCupid surveyed its users, and that's what they discovered.

Forty-six percent of men think they are geniuses.

This suggests that male clients think they are smarter than we are. They're geniuses, after all, and genius is rare.

This explains why I always caution women never to appear uncertain with a male client. Prone to believing themselves smarter than anyone, male or female, most male clients pounce on providers who waver in their advice, and even harder if someone is in a negotiation. Men prey on uncertainty.

This is also why advisors should wear black or dark blue to meetings with male clients. Those are the colors deliberately chosen by judges and Supreme Court justices, police officers, umpires, airline captains, and presidents. Their good reason for choosing those colors is yours, too.

So stick to your guns.

Talk Like Smart Travelers Walk

One of my clients teaches "security." It's a loose term in the industry, given that some of their training is in hand-to-hand fighting. But another part of the training may sound startling to you.

It's in walking.

My client discovered that criminals choose their targets by their walks. So my client teaches people how to walk: head and shoulders up, back, and with decisive steps. It echoes the twist on Theodore Roosevelt's famous advice: to walk tall and carry a big stick.

All animals do what criminals do. Hunting packs look for the weakest in the herd before they pounce. These hunters are not looking for a fight. They want easy prey and a quick meal.

If my clients advised business advisors, they would teach them how to talk: head up and decisive. Don't waver. Like all animals, humans prey on uncertainty and look for the smallest hints of it.

Save your doubts for the drive home.

But What About Humility?

You cannot work in the world of finance and investing without knowing the rules of decision-making, nicely put forth in former treasury secretary Robert Rubin's 1999 commencement address at the University of Pennsylvania. And the first rule is the Rule of Doubt:

The only certainty is that there is no certainty.

Total confidence in any advice is foolish. But that isn't the point. It brings us to his next point:

Despite uncertainty, we must act.

"He who hesitates is lost." A well-considered action is better than none. A non-decision won't answer the client's need or cure his problem. It will only prolong it.

All decisions are a matter of weighing probabilities.

You are not promising a great outcome. You are recommending what is most likely to produce an excellent one.

So, if you reacted to the previous advice on decisiveness with "only fools are certain," you are right. But I am not arguing for certainty. I am advocating for confidence and the importance of projecting it, particularly given that the signal trait of every client for a service is—once more—*fear, uncertainty, and doubt.*

You cannot add to those fears. You must allay them.

The previous advice may suggest that you should never be uncertain. You should always be. But you have weighed the probabilities and recommended what is most likely to produce an excellent outcome. That's all anyone can do.

And it's precisely what you are paid for.

You must believe to be effective.

Another Myth to Resist

Recent common wisdom advises you to mimic the person's posture and movements. You shouldn't, at least not consciously. Constantly monitoring the other person's gestures and how to move to match them steals your focus from the person's words. Plus, if she has read that advice—and many people have—she may feel manipulated.

This advice also mistakes cause and effect. When two people mirror each other, it does not somehow cause better feelings between them. It's an effect of the feelings they already have.

Do this instead: *listen with your entire body.* Put your entire self into listening and you naturally will move in sync with the other person. Plus, listening with all of your body focuses you, which ensures that you will hear and retain more. Not least of all, the other person will feel engaged.

Two words can encourage you to do this, at the outset of each meeting:

All In.

Listen, all in.

Studying Happy Couples

These observations about body language overlook something that you know intuitively. On your next visit to a coffee shop or restaurant, watch the pairs of people. Without hearing a word, you know which pairs are in sync. The shoulders of the out-of-sync pairs are pinched upward, their hands often form fists, and their motions look stiff.

The people in sync look almost limp by comparison. And when they move, they flow.

Tension is your enemy in a meeting because of what it means to the other person. Tension occurs when you are hoping for a particular outcome but are worried that it will not come. The golfer tensing up over the four-foot putt to make a birdie; the speaker gripping each side of the podium with white knuckles; the person waiting for a cab and constantly checking his watch or phone for the time. Each is hoping for something they fear will not occur, and their bodies shout it: they are tense.

Appear tense, and your listener will sense you are there with an agenda and that you fear your plan will fail. You appear too eager and unsure.

Effective salespeople *never* look that way. They appear confident, at ease, and not too eager. They appear *truly interested in* the other person, and not in what the person might do for them.

Be confident, at ease, and not too eager.

The Peak End Effect and the Meeting

An inspiration for you:

You are planning a presentation to a prospect. Your due diligence reveals he was born and raised in Baltimore.

You make your pitch.

Now you know you come to the key, Peak End Moment of your pitch: the final seconds of the thanks and goodbye.

You pull it off smartly:

"As an expression of thanks for you taking the time to hear my pitch," you tell him, "I have something for you."

You reach into your bag and pull from it a nicely wrapped box. He opens it.

He removes the tissue to find a circular metal key chain emblazoned, "Baltimore Orioles."

He immediately decides you're clever, resourceful, and thoughtful, and that you take extra time in your work.

End your pitches at a peak. Leave a lasting reminder.

How to Give an Excellent Eight-Minute Presentation

The average length of a television segment has shrunk to eight minutes, and even casual TV viewers are now used to eight-minute blocks as their standard for information.

So, to write an excellent eight-minute presentation, write an excellent ten-minute presentation.

Then slash two minutes. You can, trust me. Your copy will sound crisper and all the fat will be gone, leaving only the muscle of your message.

Now cut out thirty more seconds, so you finish thirty seconds early.

When she spoke at the first TEDWomen, Courtney was given nine minutes to share her take on feminism. "It was the most important writing exercise I have ever done," she says. "Knowing I had nine minutes to say what mattered most made me get absolutely clear on what I wanted to say."

Listeners will be grateful you respected their time and impressed by the force and clarity of your message. Abraham Lincoln, it's worth noting, delivered the Gettysburg Address in less than two-and-a-half minutes.

And resist using slides. Slides all but force you to commit three sins.

First, you will be tempted to glance at your clicker and/or the slides. This diverts your eyes from your listeners, and we mistrust people who avert their eyes from us. This conviction is embodied in the parent's demand of the dissembling child, "Look me in the eyes when you say that."

Second, slides force you to darken a room. If we are less able to see you, we are less likely to warm to you.

Third, slides with text ask your audience to read the slide instead of listening to you. This works if your slide contains only an image, because we can hear words while we see an image related to those words. But if the slide contains words, we read instead of listen. We disengage from you, and you don't want this—even for a few seconds.

Finally, slides lack what all great presentations must have: emotional resonance. It is not far-fetched to imagine Martin Luther King ruining his famous speech by flashing a slide that read:

I Have a Dream
- a. Racial Equality
- b. Have Seen Promised Land
- c. Free at Last!

Make it short, then make it shorter—and as slide-free as possible.

The PowerPoint Problem

You practice the syncing.

You spend time practicing the syncing you could spend practicing delivering the message.

You worry if you have all the equipment.

You worry about the setup.

You get it right, you hope.

You start to speak.

You worry about the equipment.

It justifies your concern: it stalls.

You stop and fix it and apologize.

You worry about more glitches.

You get anxious.

You look anxious.

And distracted.

Oops. Slide out of place.

You apologize for that, too.

You look more anxious and distracted.

Your audience loses confidence. *If he isn't great at this*, they wonder, *how great can he be at his work?*

So:

Is the possible reward of your slides greater than all this risk?

PowerPoint? Probably not.

What Makes a Powerful Presentation?

An interviewer once asked the actress Rosalind Russell, "What makes a great movie?"

"Moments," she said. "If your movie has three moments that your audience remembers, it will succeed."

This principle also applies to presentations. Give your audience three moments.

One moment should touch them. Think of the proven power of the signature of American movies, the Happy Ending. Or the related story of how a person's life got better as a result of a service you performed.

Your second moment should delight them. Laughter lubricates the connecting process. But your humor shouldn't be a joke. Instead, tell a true story with a funny aspect, or show them an image that would make almost anyone laugh.

Your third moment should move your audience to act, which evokes an observation about two famous Greek leaders:

"When Aeschines spoke, everyone said, 'How well he speaks.' But when Demosthenes spoke, they said, 'Let us march against Philip.'"

So, think about your presentation differently. Think three moments: touch them, amuse them, and move them.

Does your presentation have three moments? Then you're set.

Let Them See All of You

Go to TED.com and pick out three topics that interest you. Then note which speakers most engage you. Just from osmosis, you will learn from them. And you will realize that they don't give speeches. As TED recognizes by its use of the word "talks," a great speaker talks.

Now notice something about each of those talks. What was missing in each one?

It was a lectern. There wasn't one.

To appreciate the lectern's influence, imagine a concert where the singers sing from behind lecterns. That concert would not feel the same to you, and a talk from behind a barrier doesn't, either.

Your audience wants to see you. Our bodies speak volumes, and your movements become the dance that accompanies your songs. As an added plus, moving around helps settle your butterflies.

Talk like the TEDs. Remove the barriers between you and the listener.

Forget Perfect, Focus on Passion

Bob Dylan is one of the most famous and successful singer/songwriters in the history of music, but he never could have succeeded just on his pipes. Dylan often sounds like his lungs are storing pea gravel, yet his songs have struck chords inside millions of listeners.

Similarly, Vladimir Horowitz was known for his mistakes, but his passion helped to make him one of his century's most popular pianists.

So your words matter. But just as with a song, they aren't the true heart of a talk. Your heart is. A passionate speaker can fumble a few sections, but if she conveys passion, her audience shares it.

There's actually a problem with speaking flawlessly. To err is human, and to speak without error sounds less human. This is supported by recent research that discovered that salespeople who make occasional errors in speaking far outperform those who deliver with perfect fluency.

I'm reminded of a speaker who gives the identical precise speech, word-for-memorized word, everywhere. Yvon Douran, a leading speaker's agent, offered the consensus view of agents and audiences:

"I've seen her video. It sounds soulless."

Forget perfection; show them your heart.

The Eyes Have It

It's ancient wisdom: our eyes are the windows to our souls.

It's the foundation of one of the fundamental rules of American jurisprudence: the Rule Against Hearsay. With only well-defined exceptions, a statement by someone not made in the presence of the jury cannot be admitted into evidence. The jury must be allowed to see the person, because seeing a person is all that allows the jury to trust them. They need to look the person in the eyes.

We mistrust people who won't look us in the eyes—even if our eyes are among over two hundred sets in a room.

If you look each person in an audience in the eye for a few seconds, you make each person feel important—a feeling that every person craves. It also makes each audience member feel involved; it feels to them like a conversation rather than a recitation.

Look them in the eyes.

A Test That Will Change How You Present

Try this test.

I tell you something and look away. I add something more and look away. And I add one more thing and look away.

What is your feeling?

It's that I was not telling you the truth, particularly if I looked to the left in each case.

Now, what happens if you present to me using slides? You say something to me, then look away. Indeed, a slide presentation involves a series of comments and looks away.

A prospect only will choose someone he can trust. If you did not trust me in the test above, will a prospect choose you if you present with slides?

Look them in the eyes—without exception. Eliminate your slides.

What Really Impresses Listeners

Your listeners don't want to be impressed. They want to be respected.

Rookie speakers feel tempted to impress an audience, assuming that this will make their ideas sound impressive, too. But if your words or actions suggest "I am better than you," people won't care what you say.

This principle also underlies another rule of effective speaking: dress like your audience, but just a little bit better.

Don't strive to impress your listeners. Try to respect them.

Social Media & Your Website

The Social Media Starter Kit

Today, this is critical: you need to be findable.

And you want people, after finding you, to conclude you are current and successful.

Here's what you need to do. It's fast and simple.

Go to LinkedIn.com and Twitter.com.

Set up your account on each site. The founders make their billions by making this simple for everyone.

Craft a three-to-five word "professional headline" summary for LinkedIn, and an up-to-twenty-word headline for Twitter, right under "Photo" on "Profile."

These headlines will show up whenever someone searches for your name.

For photos on each one, use the identical, very professional, head-shot-only photo that you use on your website. This photo is your logo. Keep it consistent.

Now, edit your website bio, copy it, and paste it in LinkedIn's "Experience."

Finally, include a link to your business website on both sites.

Then fill in all the other stuff.

You're set up. Now you are more findable and appear current and successful.

Now you want to look one step better . . .

At least every other day, share the same article of interest to your prospects on both LinkedIn and Twitter. (Each site gives you clear instructions for this and it quickly becomes second nature.)

After several weeks, you will appear informed and informative to your prospects.

It's that easy.

Be findable, look current, sound informed—in minutes.

A Second Step

Look up all of your clients on Twitter and LinkedIn. (The search box for this looks like Google's, and is conspicuous on each first page.)

Hit "Follow" on that person's Twitter heading, to link to that client. Ideally, each client will follow you back.

Hit "Connect" on LinkedIn. In the invitation form that pops up, delete their standard invitation request—it sounds impersonal—and invite each client to link to you.

Those who follow you back on Twitter and accept your LinkedIn invitation now will be able to see the articles you share and any good news that you post regarding your business. They'll see you are staying current in your field, and each one will get a regular helping of value-added service from you several times a week.

One step—instant added value.

The Clout of Content

The last decade has echoed from the buzz about an apparently new idea: content marketing.

The idea is older than anyone reading this.

John Deere began publishing *The Furrow*, a magazine for farmers, over 120 years ago.

McKinsey & Company has often resembled a publisher with an international consulting subsidiary.

Forty years ago, Nike started publishing the magazine *Running,* which featured articles by Ken Kesey (*One Flew Over the Cuckoo's Nest*) and Hunter S. Thompson (*Fear and Loathing in Las Vegas.*)

Over thirty years ago, International Paper created two-page ads filled with expert advice. Kurt Vonnegut Jr. told readers "How to write with style," George Plimpton penned "How to make a speech," and Malcolm Forbes advised readers "How to write a business letter." Copy at the end of each ad invited readers to request reprints. Over twenty-six million people did.

Eight thousand business advisors a year publish a book, hoping the books will sell but more certain they will attract new clients.

How well does this form of marketing work? It works well for many authors and speakers, whose entire business is providing content. It would be hard for this author to suggest it cannot work spectacularly.

But businesses are less sure. At last reading, only 21 percent were certain their content marketing efforts brought in more than they cost.

But there's a catch. Writing on your area of expertise actually works well. You might even say it's a necessity.

Let's look at this.

First, you will learn that you don't merely write what you know. *You write what you learn as you write.* You see patterns you had never seen before and produce new insights.

Writing is learning. The first, second, and third reasons to write isn't to share your knowledge; it's to acquire it.

Second, you will crystallize your thinking. Ideas will come to you that would never have come to you had you not simply sat down and started.

Third, you rewrite. Writing is thinking, and rewriting is rethinking. You ask, "Does this say what I mean to say?" You answer no and keep going. You edit and realize you did more than just write more clearly; you have thought more clearly.

You've made your ideas better and more useful, and that will make you appear more authoritative.

Finally, while death and taxes are famous for being two of the certainties in life, unexpected consequences are the third. You write and, as happened for me over twenty years ago, things happen.

Often, very good things.

Write. It makes you better at what you do.

But About What?

Now, what should you write about?

You decided what you should write when you completed your Target, Evidence, Claim statement.

Laser-focus on information on your specialty, which your targets will want to know and benefit from reading about, which will reinforce your claim of expertise. Those articles will grow into a collection, clearly branded under your name, that your prospects, when they do internet searches on the topic, are apt to find.

Focus your writing, too—like a laser.

From Author to Authority

We have established that clients want to work with experts. And what do experts do?

Most do what this author did. We worked our way up slowly.

In 1990, relying on my six years as an attorney and many more in marketing, I wrote an article on legal marketing and submitted it to *Minnesota Law & Politics*. The rest is a revealing history.

One of my first clients had a younger brother who was dating an attorney in one of the twin cities' largest firms. She noticed my name on the article and read it, then copied it and placed it on the desk of the firm's marketing partner, Clifford Greene. The article impressed him enough to call me and begin a lifetime as my client, friend, and, eventually, my best man.

My writing career—and I write this for your inspiration—might have ended there. But two years later, Cliff called me with a second challenge: from his synagogue. They had been toiling on a strategic plan for over a year and were basically running in place.

Cliff was concerned and weary.

"Do you have any advice?" he asked. I wasn't sure but suggested we meet for lunch.

Over lunch, I offered some reasons why planning so often fails. He liked what I said and asked if I would share my thoughts with the temple's committee.

I wrote my ideas into a script, which I presented, to a favorable reaction. And that, too, could have been the end of it, but an accident happened. The day after my presentation, a designer named Sue Crolick asked me to review one of her talks, this for the American Institute of Graphic Arts local chapter. I agreed and listened to her, wrote suggestions on several pieces of paper I'd grabbed off my desk, and left her those notes.

The next morning, I learned that people actually do "burst" through doors. Sue burst through mine.

"What was that on the back of your notes for me?" she asked.

"There was something on the back?"

"Yes, something about planning."

I'd obviously written my notes on the back of my speech to Cliff's group.

"Oh, that must have been my presentation to Temple Israel."

"Well, you must get it published," Sue said. "It was terrific."

So I copied the speech and sent it to another local business publication. They published it and ended up receiving complimentary letters from five different states. That naturally inspired the editor, Jay Novak, to ask if I had any other ideas.

"I may," I told him at lunch shortly after the planning article appeared. "I specialize in services, and they aren't like products. They're invisible. So I might write about that. I'd call the article 'Selling the Invisible.'"

"That's it!" Jay said.

After the article appeared, the response prompted another request, which I answered with a sequel. This time, the Twin Cities' top literary agent saw the article and phoned me.

"Do you have more stuff?" he said. "You might have a book here."

And thus, one article begat a speech, which begat a mistake, which eventually begat a book. And another and another, among other welcome but unintended consequences.

Write—and watch what can happen.

Niche Master, Not Thought Leader

Beginning in early 2009, a smart Chicago labor law attorney saw The Affordable Care Act coming. By the time the legislation passed in

March 2010, was upheld by the Supreme Court of the United States in June 2012, and was ready for initial rollout in October 2013, few private attorneys had studied it more—or had so carefully thought through its implications—than Judith Wethall, whose clients needed what she could to do to help them.

Judith Wethall is a shareholder in the nationally known labor law firm Littler. And Judith is something different from, and better than, a Thought Leader.

She's a Niche Master who gets things done for her clients in the niche of labor law.

Few clients want Thought Leaders. In the last thirty-five years, American businesses have widely and successfully adopted only six Thought Leader ideas: benchmarking, business process reengineering, balanced scorecard, Six Sigma, knowledge management, and customer relationship management, and four of those six ideas depend primarily on ideas dating back to the 1950s and even the early twentieth century.

Clients do not want leading thoughts. They want results. Period.

You don't want me to write about the history of motivational theory, for example. You want to finish this book with some understanding and ideas of new steps you can take to attract and keep clients. You want reading this book to produce results.

So forget trying to become a Thought Leader, whatever that might be. Be a Judith. Be the Niche Master.

Consider, after all, what the word "thought" tends to connote:

"*Here are my thoughts on this.*" Thoughts are speculative, initial, and tentative.

"*I thought you were bringing the burgers and I was bringing the chips.*" Thoughts are mere understandings and often are mistaken.

"*People once thought the earth was flat.*" Thoughts often prove to be comically wrong.

In addition, Americans tend not to trust mere thinking. We believe that most brilliant thinkers are eccentrics who think big thoughts but cannot find their cars in a parking lot. Voters in the US once disparaged a presidential candidate for just that reason; they called Adlai Stevenson an "egghead," and elected a man of action instead: the Supreme Commander of the Allied Forces in Europe, Dwight D. Eisenhower.

We are doers, not thinkers. We want action, not ideas.

We care about what works, not about the mysteries of beauty and truth. Indeed, three Americans—Charles Sanders Peirce, William James, and John Dewey—are known as the founders of Pragmatism, a philosophy so practical some people dispute whether it should even be called a philosophy. It often reads like mere cost-benefit analysis.

And we all know this: leading thoughts rarely are accepted at first. They sound unfamiliar, which makes us uncomfortable. The great Thought Leader on quality, W. Edwards Deming, was virtually unrecognized in our country, but was lauded in Japan. He remained essentially unknown in the US until NBC aired a white paper, "If Japan Can, Why Can't We?" on June 24, 1980. On that night, Deming was eight months past his eightieth birthday.

Arthur Schopenhauer put the problem perfectly. "All truths pass through three phases. First, it is ridiculed. Second, it is violently opposed. Third, it is accepted as self-evident." Thinking well can simply put you decades ahead of the curve.

Forget thoughts, then. "Thought" is a weak word, and thoughts are not what clients want. Clients may read thinkers, but they hire doers.

Be a Judith.

The Mother of All Marketing Vehicles

You go to a website. It's pretty good. But some links are slow. Or you notice a grammatical mistake, like "Its time!" instead of "It's time!"

Do you think, *This isn't a very good website*?

No. You think, *This isn't a very good company.*

Your prospects think that, too.

That experience demonstrates that, in this new digital world, you are your website.

Make yours right—and remarkable.

The Golden Rectangle

The figure on the next page may remind you of that childhood pastime of connecting the dots. But it's vital to understanding what makes an effective website.

First, take a pen and draw a rectangle that connects each of the four periods.

Look at that rectangle. It's 5.8 inches high and 2.8 inches wide: the total screen area of the iPhone 13.

Now consider this. A growing number of prospects, including for you, search on their phones. If their search leads them to your website, all they see is what fits on that ten-plus-inch-square rectangle.

What you put in that rectangle is an inexpensive but important advertisement for you. But like the inexpensive ads you might place in a neighborhood shopper, it doesn't allow you much space to state your claim and coax a reader to take the next step.

So, to optimize your website, ask, "What words and image can I squeeze into that space that are most likely to get a reader to act?"

What is your Killer Headline?

Is it big enough to be read easily?

Is the image big enough and clear enough to be read easily, too? Is it critical to your message?

Does the image deliver a compelling message? Does it lead some readers to think you can make their lives a little better—perhaps much better?

Here.   Here.

Here.   Here.

Perfect this message. It's the message you want to deliver repeatedly and in every communication. This is your elevator speech, on what admittedly is a quick ride from the first floor to the second.

Get your entire killer message on your prospects' phone screens.

Bells and Whistles, or Noise?

When a website tries to dazzle you with its special effects, what are its owners hiding?

Research by CEB confirms every reader's experience: more stuff doesn't work. Tell your reader what he needs to know, and then stop.

CEB found that companies that simplify our decision-making are 86 percent more likely to make a sale.

Offering more—more flashes and dashes and more information— doesn't work. The average American sees several thousand marketing messages every day. Flashier won't work when so many are flashing.

Web users scan and skim. Only 16 percent read every word on your page. Seventy-nine percent simply scan your page.

What does that scanner see on a quick scan? What is your compelling message? How can you make someone's life a little better? Can they see your claim immediately?

Silence the bells and whistles.

A Key to a Credible Website

Here's a quiz question only one person has ever answered correctly:

What element of a website most influences a reader to decide if you are credible?

Client testimonials?

Case studies showing proven success?

Your biography and the credentials and accomplishments?

A scientist, BJ Fogg—and, not incidentally, one of *Fortune* magazine's "Ten New Gurus You Should Know"—decided to study this in 2002. He invited 2,684 average people to view over 100 different websites in 10 different content areas. When he and his team with the Stanford Web Credibility Project studied the results, they were surprised.

"I would like to think website visitors are very tough integrators of information," said Fogg, "but the truth is—and I didn't want to find this but the research is very clear:

"People judge the credibility of a web site by how it looks."

The Ideal Website and the Hearsay Rule

Seeing is believing. We believe our eyes more than anything else. We know they help us evaluate what we see and the people we meet.

"He saw it with his own eyes," we say about an eyewitness. "It must be true."

This again confirms the reason for the famous Hearsay Rule. A statement made outside of the court is generally not admissible. The jurors deciding the case must be able to see the person making the statement so they can accurately assess the credibility. Seeing him is believing—or disbelieving—him.

This relates to another form of testimony: the testimonials on your website. They can work, but readers often mistrust them.

Readers ignore anonymous testimonials and often assume the statements are made up. Readers also deeply distrust semi-anonymous testimonials (e.g., "William, Los Angeles" or "Catherine, Miami").

Unfortunately, and as another result of this digital age, most readers mistrust signed testimonials, too. You cannot read many Amazon reader reviews, for example, without assuming that several five-star reviews must come from the author's friends.

Not least of all, these reviews are hearsay. We only "hear" what that reviewer "says." So we do not fully trust them.

So what do you do with testimonials on your site?

At a minimum, include the person's photo alongside her testimonial. Let us see the person testifying.

Ideally, go two steps further: film the testimonial if possible. That the client was willing to take the time offers a testimony by itself. If the client looks enthusiastic, trustworthy, and even impressive, all the better.

It's true of testimonials, too.

Don't just say you have testimonials. Show them.

Video and the Celebrity Problem

Every day on a Zoom meeting is a bad hair day.

That is because when we appear on video, we suffer from the Celebrity Effect. As amateurs, we cannot compete with the professionals who appear on television and in film. Or with their teams of hairstylists, makeup artists, and lighting experts.

So, if and when you perform on video, you are competing with *The Today Show* and *The View*. Those men and women are professionals being filmed in a TV studio by top professionals. We are not.

And research supports another problem with revealing yourself on video: people have less favorable views of people they see on video than of people they meet face-to-face.

As a marketing tool, think twice before you show a video of yourself.

The Power of Reviews in an Age of Hype

Researchers once gave a group of human resources professionals a resume and a letter of recommendation for each of two job candidates, John and David.

These resumes and letters were identical, except for eight words added to David's letter: "David can sometimes be challenging to work with."

Which candidate did the HR people find most appealing?

David. Because his recommendation included an apparent criticism of him, the readers were more apt to trust the writer's praise of him.

This phenomenon also has been suggested by a study at Boston University's Questrom School of Business. Daniella Kupor, an assistant professor of marketing, gave volunteers a chance to buy a product with a glut of five-star reviews. But the four-star review persuaded 19 percent more people to buy. Because it was willing to mention a weakness in the product, the volunteers were more apt to trust the reviewer's praise of its strengths.

Are your claims and testimonials too good to feel true?

The Three-Word Website Test

It's among the famous axioms of advertising: "The best way to kill a bad product is with great advertising."

Great ads lead people to try the product, discover it's bad, and spread the bad word.

The same applies if you drive dozens of readers to a third-rate website. They scan the site and never return.

So, before you try to drive people to your website, make sure it's remarkable. Otherwise, your website will undermine all your marketing efforts.

But easier said than done, you say. How do you know when your site is right?

It's simple: it's "*ICE.*"

The ideal website conveys *Immediate Compelling Evidence.*

It offers *Evidence*: provable facts—three are ideal—that suggest you must be very good at what you do.

It's *Immediate*: readers find that evidence within five seconds.

And it's *Compelling*: it's strong, and readers trust and believe it.

Is your website icy? One in ten are. Chances are you are among the other nine.

And chances are, we can fix this in the next few pages.

Make your website icy.

The World's Most Effective Website Writers

The clever and skilled veterinarians for BluePearl have created one of the world's most effective websites.

The BluePearl site doesn't flash or bedazzle, but it's hard to imagine a pet owner visiting the site and not thinking, *These veterinarians are really good.*

That's not because of what the veterinarians say. It's what their clients have written. Knowing their clients' enthusiasm for BluePearl, the veterinarians invite them to submit their stories for a section titled "Your Stories."

If you love animals, the headlines draw you in like clickbait: "Adele Swallowed a Fishing Hook" and "Skeletor the Cat Saved by Dr. He-Man" are personal favorites.

There's also the poignant headline that reminds us of pets' special place in our lives: "Happy Is My Only Family Member."

You can read just the headlines, written by BluePearl's customers, and conclude that this may be the region's premier veterinary service.

And the best web copy was written by clients.

What if your clients wrote on your site?

Why Video Is Smart

It's simple: Google owns the site where videos appear; Google owns YouTube.

After spending $1,650,000,000 on that purchase, the people at Google want people to watch videos. So their search engine gives special treatment to videos.

And Twitter reports that if you include a video in a tweet, it's 28 percent more likely to be shared than a text-only tweet.

This cozy relationship, forged in 2006, improves the chances of your video being seen and boosts your page rank on Google. It moves you up nearer the top, where you want to be. So, if you have the resources to create a video, and can produce one that looks as professional as it can be within your budget, it can dramatically improve the visibility of your service.

The general rule is that videos increase the chances of a tweet being retweeted.

And it is possible that videos of a business owner are retweeted at the same rate. But that does not assure a good outcome; it may merely mean that more people get to see the business owner muddle her or his way through. Business owners do not tend to be accustomed to, and skilled at, performing on camera, and because of that there is a risk that a video of the business owner will actually do more harm than good.

An example: My first speeches were so bad that a client/friend politely encouraged me to avoid them. Several performances later, I was good at it, and in 2005 I was named one of world's five best speakers in a survey conducted by the speaking agency Speaker's Platform.

Video gives sites a boost.

Almost Everything You Need to Know About SEO

Search engine optimization—employing every possible device to move your website onto Google's first page—isn't for amateurs.

That's because SEO is really GO: Google optimization. Google dominates search, and if you want to appear on the first page of Google, you need to optimize for it. And that's the challenge.

Google hires brilliant people to ensure that Google is a reliable source of, and filter for, the most valuable information on every topic. Google's ability to consistently get you to the best and most credible information on a given subject is what makes Google Google, and what makes it worth tens of billions. Its success depends on it.

Which means that every time a sneak devises a way to trick Google, the engineers at Google retaliate. They must find, and do find, a way to foil the ruse.

So Google constantly changes its algorithms to make sure that ruses don't work.

You cannot keep up with these changes. Only an expert SEO company can.

So, if you believe you can benefit from SEO, hire an expert.

They are out there, and the honest ones will help you. But like all good expert advice, it isn't cheap.

So this is all you really need to know about SEO:

Don't do it yourself.

The Second Thing You Must Know

There is no point in trying to optimize for search engines if your information is ordinary.

Because rising onto the first page of Google, so that hundreds of people will come to your site and read your information, is useless if the readers decide, "Not much here." Or even worse, "This isn't any good."

Just as great advertising is known for its ability to kill a bad product, great SEO is the best way to undermine a poor website, and the reputation you hoped to improve with your content.

Great marketing communications in any medium—social, print advertising, brochures—start with great communication: a powerful message of value to the reader, delivered clearly, crisply, and well. It's a variation of how McCann Erickson distilled its skill at advertising into its simple three-word theme:

"Truth well told."

To optimize your website, optimize its message.

The Third Thing

A brilliantly written ad for a New York ad agency back in the early '80s coaxed me from law into advertising.

I think I can repeat it here verbatim, decades after reading it:

Nothing worthwhile comes easily. Half efforts do not produce half results, they produce no results. Work—hard work, constant work, relentless work—is the only way to produce results that last.

So it is with all social media marketing and with SEO. Results do not come right away. They take months. And after those months, all those new visitors to your website still may not be turning into clients. They are merely readers. You still may need to do more to persuade them to contact you. And even then, they may not become clients.

There are no shortcuts. My client Gary Cohen appears on the first page under a Google search for "Minnesota Executive Coach."

He spent ten years and over $240,000 on editors and an SEO consultant to get there.

"And it didn't really show a return until the fifth year," Gary has told me.

Hard work—and, in the case of SEO, your hard dollars invested in a good SEO firm—is the only way to achieve results.

And there is one more challenge:

The rules change constantly. So, what optimizes your site this spring may not work this fall. That means you must optimize as an ongoing process rather than a one-week cleanup. You need to budget time and dollars for it on an ongoing basis.

If you can afford that, and if you can live without knowing the results for months, you should invest in SEO. If not, you should invest in other marketing efforts that still work.

And may work even better.

SEO is not a shortcut. And it may not even be a route.

Banner Ads

You notice those tiny ads on websites and wonder, "Why do they bother?"

And marketers hear this, too: "Banner ads don't work. Click-through rates are awful."

Yet banner ad sales are up. Analyst eMarketer recently doubled its online ad spending projections for the year and predicted that display ads soon will overtake search ads as the biggest online ad segment.

And people wonder why Facebook is worth so many billions? It's because Facebook's revenue is driven by banner ads.

Are banner ads a waste?

No. Click-through isn't the only measure of a banner ad's effect, as several studies suggest.

This is another example of the Mere Exposure Effect: merely being exposed to something several times makes you like that thing more.

That's why banner ads, often with nothing but a name, work. They make us feel comfortable with what is being advertised, even when we cannot recall the ad.

As noted elsewhere, familiarity breeds liking.

Banner ads also work because they say so little, and not in spite of it. A banner ad gives us little to digest and little to compete for our attention. So the name is more apt to register and stick, and cause us to like whatever is being advertised. It's not because that product or service has a feature or benefit that we like—other than the feature of having a name that we know and feel more familiar with.

A successful ad can say almost nothing? Well, no one clicks on the NASCAR cars streaming by or golf pros sauntering by, each festooned with nothing more than logos on their cars and golf shirts. But these ads work.

Just ask the golfer Phil Mickelson, who earns almost $50 million a year just for wearing them.

Ads that say only your name often say just enough.

The Limit—and Irony—of Social Media

Social media appeals to people who most need true social marketing— which is socializing. It's getting face-to-face with prospects and influencers.

You can prove this for yourself. Do you ever buy a service—as opposed to a product—from someone whose face you see on Facebook or Twitter? No. You buy from people you see over coffee, or whom you met once at a party.

The most effective media for marketing a service, like a service itself, are those that put you face-to-face with prospects.

People have to see you to choose you. If you are focusing on using social media because you want to avoid the socializing that builds a service business, you are doing the third-best thing for the first-worst reason.

The most powerful social marketing is just that: face-to-face.

The Easy Sure Things

Email makes it easy to cold-call thousands of people, but the ease of doing it all but guarantees its failure.

We love easy solutions, especially the ones sold to us as sure things. You read about fifty Surefire Headlines, for example—which were sure things until several thousand people read about them and started recycling them endlessly. The headline "You are not alone," once famous for working, is now passé. We've heard it so often it's white noise; we no longer hear it at all.

Look at your inbox tonight. How many of those emails will you end up reading?

If you are looking for easy, you can't beat email. If you are looking for clients, try something harder.

The Peak End Rule and Your Email

Again and again, the Peak End Rule reminds us that how we finish anything—a movie, a piece of music, a presentation—really matters. People most remember the endings.

How do your emails end? Craft the lines after your name to capture the same message in your Key Evidence Statement: recognition, achievements, and credentials. Every time someone sees your email, you want to reinforce your strong qualifications.

And include with your email the same photo that appears on your website and LinkedIn and Twitter profiles. You want to emblazon that photo—it's your logo—into everyone's mind.

End your emails at a peak, too.

Seven Tips from the World's Most Successful Marketer

Everything that Procter & Gamble has learned over the last seventy years from relentlessly testing every ad and commercial it produces applies in every medium you use—your website, Facebook, advertisements, everything.

P&G and the other huge packaged goods companies in America got huge—and very profitable—by figuring out what works in television and print ads, and what doesn't. They test and retest endlessly—and have been doing so for decades. These are some key lessons they learned.

1. People love animals, especially dogs—and puppies even more.
2. Jokes don't work, but situational humor does—a little levity goes a long way, and makes you appear more human. Jokes are very much a matter of taste, but humor tends to be universal.
3. You can't scare us into doing anything. States tried for years to do just that, showing us horrifying images of the results of car crashes in which the occupants failed to buckle their seat belts. These pictures actually triggered what is called reactance: we—particularly men—hate to be told what to do. Do this or you'll die actually proved to encourage more people *not* to fasten their seat belts. It's only when we were given a choice—you can either buckle up or not (and get a ticket)—that seat belt advertising finally worked.

4. No one runs ads without pictures. Images add to interest and retention. Always include a photo in every marketing communication. If it's a long piece, add extra photos to break up the long blocks of copy.

5. People hear what they see. What they remember is what they saw, not what they heard—unless you repeat it at least twice. Images stick immediately, but words take much longer.

6. Logos work because logos are images. A distinctive signature for your company sticks in our mind, but your name alone doesn't. Unless it's so odd it's unforgettable.

   This is why advertising clients always insist, "Make the logo bigger." We copywriters hated it because we wanted to create something really cool-looking, and big logos get in the way and steal our thunder. Even more important for our selfish purpose, award-show judges—who are art directors and writers, not incidentally—dislike big logos. People who buy things don't necessarily love big logos, either, but those images stick in people's minds.

7. People like lists. A lot.

And Seven More, with Thanks to Procter & Gamble

1. We love real news. If it's new, tell us. If it's new information, share it—and tell us it's new. Keep us up to date. We love feeling that we are on top of things, even little ones. Like why the current power couple broke up. However . . .

2. We hate being tricked. If it's not new, if it won't change our life forever, if it won't make our jaw drop, don't tell us that it will. Fool us once, shame on you. Fool us twice—you can't. We won't give you the chance.

3. Comparing yourself to others simply does not work. Comparison ads have been tried and tried—and have failed and failed. Pepsi tried to challenge Coke for years and ended up selling more Coca-Cola for Coca-Cola and less Pepsi for Pepsi. Deloitte tried to beat its leading competitors by making comparisons to them, by name. It did not go well and the company then had to send out a spokesperson, nationwide, to apologize for it. Microsoft tried to do this against Apple; that backfired horribly, too.

4. Stand on your two feet; don't try to knock your competitors' feet out from under them. It will only trip you.

5. We love solutions. We know we have challenges; we want to overcome them. "How to" headlines work wonderfully. However . . .

6. People have so abused the proven headlines—including "How to"—that you need to avoid those words. "Seven Steps to Solving" or something similar works better. However . . .

7. Seven is the limit. Remember the Magic Rule of Seven (Plus or Minus Two): we can't remember more than seven things, and eight sounds like it takes too long. *The 7 Habits of Highly Effective People* worked well. But Covey was pushing the limit—it was a well-conceived and -argued book, and it's over thirty years old. Things were a littler simpler then..Seven is good but five works better. Plus you can save your other two good ideas for two separate articles.

And for reasons no one can figure out, odd numbers seem to work better than even ones.

Final Thoughts on Persuading

Four Thoughts on Communicating

1. Your most significant competitor is your prospect's indifference.
2. Do not communicate just to be understood. Communicate so that you cannot be misunderstood.
3. Don't say it; prove it.
4. Fewer words, better words; compelling writing has no fat.

Six Reminders on Your Message

1. We've heard it all before. You must say something new.
2. To make me trust that you are different, sound different.
3. Conventional messages do not produce conventional results. They produce no results.
4. Make every moment of your message worth our while, or we will never listen to another one.
5. If you need forty seconds to convince me, I will choose someone who takes twenty.
6. You need a sharp point to pierce a person's resistance.

RELATING

Dare to Be Good

During my avid running years, reading a Nike ad was like chatting with another avid runner. Nike knew me, and I felt connected to their brand because of it.

Their ads accomplished what Dan Wieden, the head of their agency, said is the goal of all great marketing communication: to establish "a provocative relationship between good companies and their customers."

There are two key words in Dan's comments.

If you are promoting a service, you are offering a relationship. But, as with another person, a person can only have a good relationship with a good company.

For your marketing to be good, you must be.

From my observation, the outstanding service provider shares the four key traits of my exceptional clients. They have been empathetic women and men of extraordinary integrity who love their work and are constantly open to the possibility that they might be wrong: they embody empathy, integrity, love, and humility. I understand the temptation to add talent but have never known anyone who combined those four traits yet lacked the talent needed to perform their job well.

To communicate more effectively with your prospects, become better: more honest, more humble, more open, more revealing. Tell them why you love what you do.

Don't thump your chest; reveal the heart inside it.

To market better, become better.

The Price He Paid

In 1991, a poll of American architects recognized Frank Lloyd Wright with an assessment he would have considered disparaging; they named him the greatest American architect of all time.

In a courtroom more than half a century before, Wright was asked to identify himself before testifying and said, "I am the world's greatest architect." The attorney asked how he could say that.

"I have to," Wright said. "I am under oath."

Not many years later, the architect decided he had understated his stature when he testified, "I actually am the greatest architect in the history of the world."

He may have been. A poll of architects in 1986 that named the ten greatest American buildings named three of his: the iconic Fallingwater home outside Pittsburgh, the Robie House in Chicago, and the SC Johnson Wax Administration Building in Racine, Wisconsin. No other architect was credited with more than one.

But this undisputed master was a problematic person. One client wrote to complain of a leaky roof—a problem for which Wright became infamous—and mentioned that the leak presented a particular nuisance because it was splashed onto his desk.

Wright wrote back, "Move your desk."

In an era that insisted a man should not covet his neighbor's wife, Wright coveted more than one and paraded with the first in their Oak Park, Illinois, neighborhood. The word spread. Again and again.

And then there was Wright's wrath, which he unleashed on everyone: his entire profession, lawyers, contractors, bankers, and even his clients' wives.

Pride, lust, and wrath: in a book on the Seven Deadly Sins, Wright could take up three chapters. And if vanity was added as an eighth, a single photo of Wright in one of his flamboyant capes and flowing neckties might eliminate any need for accompanying copy.

But his genius is beyond doubt. I was only thirteen and could see it. I remember reading about him in *Life* magazine. The photos of Fallingwater and Taliesin immediately inspired my several-year obsession with Kenner Girder and Panel sets.

But was his unmatched talent and passion enough? He lived in constant debt, and foreclosures and the threats of them left him homeless more than once. From 1900 to 1909, before his affair in Oak Park became public knowledge, he had ninety commissions. In the ten years that followed, he had only twenty-nine.

And consider this. When Fallingwater, the SC Johnson building, and his fourth iconic creation, the Guggenheim Museum in New York City, were completed, he was seventy, seventy-two, and ninety-two years old, respectively. Had he lived to be only sixty-five, no one but the architects reading this would even recognize his name. And the First World War and the Roaring Twenties gave him a reprieve; Americans relaxed their stern attitudes about sex and infidelity. And with his age came more forgiveness, because what we loathe as arrogance in a younger man looks like mere eccentricity in a sixty-five-year-old, and we expect those quirks, particularly in an artist and even more in a genius.

But what might have been?

What if Wright had contained his wrath, vanity, and pride, and either reined in his lust for married women, or at least kept it from public view?

What might those thirty years between the Robie House and Fallingwater have produced?

And what commissions might he have gotten to keep his banks and creditors away and allow him to focus on his work instead of his survival?

His work was admired, even revered, but the man was not. And he paid for it.

We sometimes read about the cost of caring too much about what others think. But doesn't the story of Frank Lloyd Wright suggest the cost of caring too little?

Once more: To market better, be better.

Performing Is Marketing

Several years ago, I asked my oldest son, Harry IV, how he marketed his always-busy web and app development firm, Hot Pixel.

"I don't."

He did not need to explain why: he and his back-end developer whiz, Brent, do exceptional work. Their work is their marketing strategy. Delighted clients became persuasive references.

That old saying about products captures this perfectly: "Build a better mousetrap, and the world will beat a path to your door."

For decades, building better mousetraps has been the marketing strategy of Thomas Keller, the first restaurateur in America ever to head two Michelin three-star restaurants simultaneously, Per Se in New York City and the world-renowned French Laundry in the upper Napa Valley of California. Harry IV, Brent, and Mr. Keller do not market their services; they focus all their efforts on perfecting them.

To market better, look for ways to perform better.

The Power of the Experience

You spot the airline captain approaching your gate and heading to board. He's wearing dark glasses. Inside, the stewardess tells you they're serving filet mignon and free champagne. "On the flight that left for Denver an hour ago," she adds with a huge smile, followed by loud laughter from the entire plane. This is, after all, the airline with those planes with a giant Smiley Face on their fronts and a sense of humor to match.

You are on Southwest Airlines, and you are not alone. It carries more passengers every year than any airline in America. And it does not sell getting you from here to there.

It sells an experience.

You try on two pairs of jeans. Then two more. Then three more. The salesperson never stops smiling, even after you say, "Heck with it—they all make my butt look big!" "I should be so lucky! I want yours!" she says. And she finds you three more pairs, always smiling

You sense you are the only customer in the store. You're in Nordstrom, and Nordstrom doesn't sell clothes. It sells the experience of shopping for them.

You're at Cheers bar. You come back every night. You're not buying the beer or the bartenders, even the handsome one who looks like Ted Danson, the pretty blonde who looks like Shelley Long, or the funny one who looks like Rhea Perlman. You're buying what Cheers sells: the experience of a place where everybody knows your name.

If you're selling a service, you are selling the entire experience.

How is yours?

What can you add to it to make it more like Southwest, Nordstrom, or Cheers?

The fastest and least expensive way to boost your business is to improve your service. And the fastest, most memorable, and most vivid way to do that is by improving the experience.

To improve your service, improve the experience of receiving it.

Six Fallacies of Client Relationships

The Fallacy of "Customer Engagement"

My friend and I were standing in line in a Barcelona hotel when a pretty young Spanish woman asked, "How are you doing? How can I help?"

We waited twenty-six minutes. The hotel had staffed just two people to perform check-in, and five more young women to engage the frustrated people waiting helplessly in line. (At one point, I said, "Yes, you can help. Could you check us in?")

We had just flown across the Atlantic all day and night. We felt damp, frazzled, and full of cheap peanuts. The clock behind the check-in girl read 3:40. A sign below that clock promised check-in by 3:00.

When, after those twenty-six minutes, we finally got to the desk, another young woman who looked like Penelope Cruz pecked away at her keyboard and discovered our room was not ready. She smiled warmly when she said this. She smiled just as warmly seconds later when she could sense that I wanted to stab someone with one of the hotel's engaging complimentary pens.

We didn't want to be engaged. We wanted to be upstairs.

At 4:05, we finally were. Once in the room, I peeled off my sticky cotton shirt and khakis and jogged to the bathroom and into the shower. It took two minutes to decipher the nozzle. I finally showered and bounced out of the shower and began what would be a failed search for a hair dryer. We called downstairs and requested one. It arrived fifteen minutes after I called.

And it didn't work.

But those seven women from the front desk—only two of whom actually helped with check-in—certainly were engaging.

I thought of all those articles talking about the new key to success: Customer Engagement.

But companies don't engage you. Unless they offer you something wonderful.

Salespeople don't engage you. Unless they can help you.

Customer service people don't engage you. Unless they solve your problem or answer your question. Quickly.

Sleight of hand and feats of artistry engage me. Fiancées engaged me. Winning two Rose Bowls and watching two of my tee shots disappear into golf cups engaged me.

But forget all this advice about engaging your audience and clients. Neither you nor your clients have the time. Create something wondrous instead.

Make their portfolios humiliate the Dow.

Fix their problems in near real time.

Make the 6s look like 8s, somehow.

If you want to engage them while you're doing that, great. But focus, constantly, on making their life a little better.

Forget engaging; focus on helping.

What Is True Engagement?

What is one thing you'd like to see me do differently?" is exactly the question you need to ask.

It doesn't ask "What don't you like about my service?" It doesn't ask for a criticism. It invites a helpful suggestion instead.

The question also implies that the client has the insight to offer a helpful suggestion for improving your business. It's a compliment to the client.

Not least of all, the question shows you have both the courage to hear a suggestion and the desire to improve. I have heard this more than once, even from written surveys of clients asking for suggestions. At least one client in twenty writes back, "I like the mere fact you are asking me. Very few services do."

Ask this question, and you will be given two things: helpful suggestions and a client who appreciates that you cared enough to ask.

To truly engage a client, just ask one question: "What might I do differently?"

The Authenticity Fallacy

Authenticity," Christoph Niemann, the outstanding New Yorker cover illustrator, once observed, "is changing your kid's diapers. No one wants to see that."

There are no inauthentic people. There are only people who did not know how to act because they do not know who they are.

Stop bullshitting yourself and you will stop bullshitting everyone else.

Authenticity and Admirability

Typing the two words above into a Google search just scored me over 2,230,000 articles.

I hope no one is reading them.

Insisting "Be authentic" suggests you should say just what you feel. But the advice "Always think of others" does not mean "Lie when it suits you." It means choose your words carefully and consider the feelings of whomever will hear them. That advice is ageless; Castiglione captured it in *The Book of the Courtier,* almost five hundred years ago.

Like most recent business trends, the authenticity movement almost certainly arose because its advocates realized that offering the conventional, and seemingly identical, wisdom to "be honest" would not mark them as Thought Leaders. So they adopted the classic strategy: pour old wine in a new bottle and then insist the wine is new.

Be authentic? Tell a client he's greedy or rude? Appear at a nice wedding in cargo shorts and flip-flops? You should ignore any advice that minimizes the need for courtesy, the indispensable element in a civilized society. What can "civilized" mean, after all, other than to act with *civility*—a kind consideration of the feelings of others?

If it feels good, do it? No. At most given moments, we should not do what feels good or authentic, but what that situation requires.

Do your own thing, man? That is what we are back to?

No.

Be careful, but honest, and beware of the advice, "Be authentic."

The Best Practices Fallacy

There's a simple way to determine the best practice for your business: ask your client.

Mistrust anything else labeled as a best practice. What might be badass for some is simply bad for others.

The Incentives Fallacy

Twenty-one years ago, a surprise arrived in my morning mail, a package the size of a cigar box but much heavier.

An inveterate lover of surprises, I eagerly opened the box and the handsome Tiffany blue one inside it, and uncovered a beautiful, sterling silver clock. It had come from the head of a Minneapolis public relations firm to whom I had referred a client.

The clock has been on my bedside table stand for every day of the twenty-one years since that Monday morning as a constant reminder of the man's generosity.

And the reminder works: I think of his PR firm first when someone asks for a recommendation.

It is never good advice to tell your clients you will reward them for any future referrals. It actually offends many people. But always reward them. By recommending you, the client has put his reputation on the line.

Rewards, always. Incentives, never.

The Satisfied Customer Fallacy

Much of modern marketing comes from the mind of psychologist Abraham Maslow. A genius—his IQ of 190 was the second highest ever recorded—Maslow attempted to answer the classic question, "What do people want?"

But there is always more to this question of want.

As Maslow said, "The human being rarely reaches a state of complete satisfaction. As one desire is satisfied, another pops up to take its place."

This reveals the paradox of all satisfaction, including client satisfaction. Clients feel satisfied, then want more.

That means that satisfying a client isn't an act, but a series of acts. You can't rest on your laurels.

Or as Mark Twain wrote, "A human being has a natural desire to have more of a good thing than he needs."

Clients experience this constantly. The provider woos them, listens to their every word and promises and promises. The provider wins the business, and then the courtship turns into something resembling a stagnant marriage.

She loved me. Now she loves me not.

You must keep satisfying.

The Quick Fix Fallacy

From Aristotle—"a friendship is a slow ripening fruit"—to The Supremes—"you can't hurry love"—we've been reminded that friendships takes time. Creating real fans takes even longer.

You don't make a great relationship with a client. You earn one instead, a gesture at a time.

There are no fast lanes on the road to fans, who are indispensable to all marketing, acting as the advocates who relieve part of the burden of your marketing by doing some of it for you.

Yes, it takes a day at a time, but never forget this: there are a lot of days in a year.

One day at a time.

The Six Elements of
Extraordinary Relationships

The creators of internet dating sites studied relationships, of course; there was billions to be made in getting romantic relationships right. And the structure of their sites suggests how all relationships— romantic and business—progress.

First, because we hate blind dates and judge people by their faces, the dating sites require photographs. So you look at someone's photo and sense the chance of *liking*. Step one.

Next, the sites ask for a detailed profile. What is your work? Your play? And what do you value? (Asking us how we spend our time—with friends, volunteering, with our religion—reveals many of our values.)

So, what is the site trying to establish with this?

Alikeness. We enjoy people with whom we share common backgrounds, activities, and values.

What happens next on the site? If you see a person's profile and sense liking and alikeness, you send a message. If the recipient senses the same, she responds. But then, you have several back-and-forths to ensure it's worth taking the time to meet—just as a prospective client needs to do some vetting before spending time with you, given the value of time in a time-starved world like ours.

And if those several exchanged messages strengthen your initial feelings of liking and alikeness, you decide to meet.

You meet. What determines if you meet again?

Results. You both get the results from that first meeting that you hoped for.

At this stage, the parallels between dating and service-provider relationship are clear. If you like your provider, sense some alikeness, and get the results you had hoped for, you feel satisfied and you continue in the relationship.

But what is needed to deepen that relationship and eventually turn it into a commitment?

First, you decide you can rely on the person; the person acts *consistently.* Their actions are consistent with their words—they do as they promise, and they perform consistently, so that you don't fear having to deal with one person one minute and a different person the next. Their consistency gives you comfort; you know what you will get.

Second, each of you gives to the other time, effort, and perhaps gifts. You each make *sacrifices.*

And finally, you each speak and act in ways that affirm your liking. You offer *affirmations.*

These are the elements of excellent relationships: alikeness, generosity, consistency, sacrifices, and affirmations.

But let's explore these, and their implications for satisfying your clients and transforming them into delighted ones.

Element One: Alikeness

You want me to describe my most loyal clients?" my friend asked.

"Yes," I said, at lunch with a famous rainmaker.

He described two of his loyal clients. They sounded like the same person.

"Your most loyal clients sound remarkably like you," I said.

He looked down into his half-full water glass as if into a crystal ball, looking for some answers.

"I hadn't thought about it."

What his most loyal clients revealed was that likes attract. We will attract different clients over our years, but the clients who become our closest friends and fiercest advocates are those with whom we share the most in common.

A signal trait of exceptional client relationships is *alikeness*: your best clients will share much in common with you. This ends up making them comfortable; knowing that you are like them, they feel some confidence in how you will act in different circumstances. Finding these people, and nurturing your relationships with them, is a key to growing a business and making it almost self-sustaining.

The critical feeling your clients must have is alikeness.

Comfort and Alikeness

One of my favorite games with a large audience is to begin with this question:

"How many Marines are in the audience?"

At least two hands will go up. I will walk into the crowd near the closest hand and ask: "How many times have you made a sales call on another Marine and not gotten the business?"

In seventeen years, I have gotten this answer every time: "It's never happened."

In Birmingham, Alabama, I once asked a similar question of University of Alabama graduates: How many fellow Crimson Tide alumni had they called on and not gotten the business? Only one of the seven people who raised a hand had ever failed: once. When I asked, "And how many Auburn graduates have you called on and not gotten the business?" dozens of people laughed about the Crimson Tide/Auburn rivalry and a fellow in the front row piped up:

"An Alabama grad knows better than to ever try that!"

I always then add a related experience. I tell them that everyone in that audience who grew up in the state of Oregon will come up and speak to me afterward because they've learned from my presentation that I grew up there. And that common experience creates for them a sense of affinity with me, a feeling of shared common ground.

Look for common ground—your "alikeness"—with every prospect.

Alikeness and Shared Values: A Deeper Look

We just didn't have much in common."

We all have heard this often. The couple dated awhile, gave it a try, and it didn't work out. Not enough in common.

We always assume this means they didn't have enough interests in common. She golfed, he gardened; he liked country, she liked chamber music; she liked cats, and so on.

But different interests enrich relationships. The absence from a three-day fishing trip apart, for example, makes both hearts grow fonder. The relationship that goes stale, in fact, is where one or both persons do not have strong outside interests. Relationships get predictable. It's generally the same thing, every day.

But it's not only shared interests that all great relationships have in common. I discovered this four years ago when I asked, "Who of my clients have become lasting confidants, cheerleaders, and friends?"

I was sure they would be the people with backgrounds and interests very similar to mine.

But were they?

The three men and one woman were born and raised in four different time zones and none in my beloved native West. Their parents ranged from pig farmers to physicians. Only one shared my passion for pop and rock music, and the woman shook her head no at it. One attended an Ivy League school, the others large public universities. One drank beer, another scotch, one rarely, and one not at all. None shared my neurotic and sometimes sanity-threatening obsession with golf. Three were still married to their first great love. The other was in limbo.

The disconnects were so great, in fact, that I began to worry if these relationships might be more fragile than I assumed. But the shortest friendship was nearing its thirteenth birthday, and the three others were in their midtwenties.

I realized I had to look into something other than common interests and backgrounds. What else could two people have in common?

I thought, *Personality*. This was a little closer. Two extroverts, one mix, one moderate introvert. Thinkers? All four seemed to be, but Myers-Briggs and other tests suggested I was more of a Feeler than Thinker. Were there any Intuitives in the group? Two were, two weren't.

So scratch similar personalities, along with shared backgrounds and common interests. What else, then, could two people have in common? I wrote down "Beliefs and Values" and started an inventory.

Their political beliefs were identical to mine. Identical.

I then wrote down "spiritual beliefs and values."

Identical again. Every single one.

Curious, I performed this same test with my circle of closest friends.

Bingo. Five of the six shared my political beliefs and all six shared my spiritual beliefs.

Experts on marriage agree that it is not common interests or personalities that bind successful couples. *It is strongly shared values*. And it's true of all great relationships.

Now, consider the practical implications.

Where are you likely to find the people who will become these great clients, friends, and fans for life?

Where do people who share your values and beliefs gather? Shouldn't you gather with them?

Which of your clients share your values? How can you nurture those relationships for all their rewards?

Find your flock. Go where your "alikeness" is.

The Strange Force of Fake Alikeness

My first baseball bat was a Hillerich & Bradsby, Yogi Berra model.

My first putter was a Bullseye, HB (heavy blade) model.

My first tennis racquet was a Wilson HB (High Beam).

The letters "H" and "B" are my initials. I clearly am drawn to them, as if things with those initials somehow are like me.

My first "nice" wristwatch was a Bucherer. My first car was a BMW.

I wear my black Hugo Boss sport coat more than all my other coats combined. My long brown overcoat, my greatest extravagance, was made by Brioni, who also made my favorite tie and blue dress shirt.

Robert Barakett makes my four nicer T-shirts. Banana Republic makes the rest, along with my khakis and two pairs of my jeans.

My favorite classical composer is Bach, with Berlioz just behind. My favorite pieces of classical music are the *Brandenburg Concertos*, and my second and third are symphonies by Beethoven.

My favorite group in my teens were the Beach Boys, with The Beatles just behind. Only The Byrds and Beach Boys have more than two songs on my master Spotify list.

My two favorite golf courses are Bandon Trails and Bandon Dunes, and my dream course always has been Ballybunion.

When my first book was published, I asked for chapter headings in my favorite typeface, Bodoni.

The initials "HB" and letter "B" appear repeatedly in my choices and possessions. I am—and we all are—drawn to things that only seem like us. Even "fake alikeness," like things that share our initials, draw us to them.

But I am not unusual. We are unusually drawn to what seems familiar and similar to us. It's called the Name Letter Effect, and it explains why men whose last names begin with "G" are more likely to become geoscientists than those whose names begin with "T," and hardware store owners are more likely to have last names beginning with "H"—like the owner of Hoard's Hardware in my tiny town—than the letter "R."

The Name Letter Effect illustrates two things.

First—and once more—we aren't perfectly rational when we choose our clothes, baseball bats, tennis racquets, and everything else—including careers.

And we are drawn to what seems familiar and similar to us.

There are few messages in marketing more compelling than this message—express, implied, or even unstated: "I am like you."

Assure your prospects, "I am like you."

The Importance of Importance

One of the world's leading engineering consulting firms convened its national meeting in the Las Vegas backyard of one of its largest clients, the City of Las Vegas. Among the events of the fun-filled weekend was a session that many firms wisely schedule but that several partners always dread: the Client Panel. (I understand. Each time I've been asked to host one of these valuable sessions, it's been with the sense, "This is how divorce arbitrators must feel.")

A revealing event happened within the first fifteen minutes. I'll try to repeat it here verbatim from memory. I asked this of the first client:

"So, what is one thing you'd like to see KBH do differently?"

The client paused, shook his head. I saw that his face looked slightly flushed. He was hesitant but finally plowed ahead. "Okay. Three weeks ago, Jeff was in town to meet another of your clients. And I understand that you have other clients. But, umm . . ."

"Yes?"

"But he never called me. I'm sure he might not have had time for lunch, but I would have loved it if he'd just called to say, 'Hey, I'm in town and thought of you.'"

What just happened? You've just seen a vivid illustration of this basic principle of marketing a service. A service is a relationship. And it's not just a little like a relationship between friends.

It's exactly like one.

Most clients, like that fellow in Las Vegas, would like to feel like they are, if not your only client, your favorite client. You would not dream of being in their neighborhood and not calling, as only one example.

Always remember: They want to feel important to you.

Element Two: Generosity

Years ago, I prepared a commencement speech that changed my life.

Knowing I would be addressing people my children's ages, I started by asking myself: "What do I want most for my children?"

I quickly came to just three words: I wanted them to be generous, respected, and happy. That was all: three words.

Months later, I thought of that as I was writing a wedding toast for my friend Kevin. I realized that Kevin had achieved what I hoped for my children. He was respected, happy, and "the most generous man I know."

Thoughts change actions, of course, and I soon realized that thinking so much about generosity was making me more generous toward

Kevin. On many weekend mornings, I watched their one-year-old, Macklin, so Kevin and his wife, both professional night owls, could sleep in.

Kev and Meg always thanked me at least three times. I felt their regard, and it felt good.

So I found myself in the middle of my perfect triad—generosity, respect, and happiness—and began asking myself another question: Are the three intertwined? Does one—generosity—beget the others?

I was not alone in my curiosity. Notre Dame had established an institute to study generosity, psychologists and sociologists were probing it, and a professor at one of the world's most respected business schools, Wharton, wrote a *New York Times* bestseller about it.

What did all these experts think?

First, that generosity reduces stress and may even increase a person's life span.

Generosity also appears to reduce depression, but how could it not? The depressed person hears an inner voice nagging "you're not worthy." But the worthiness of an act of generosity alone negates that negative voice. When those who receive your generosity add their voices of thanks, that inner voice can only say, "Perhaps I got that wrong."

And generosity helps ensure the success of your business relationships, because, as in marriages, kindness enhances satisfaction. Great marriages thrive, above all, on kindness, and so do all great client relationships I have experienced and studied.

Ancient wisdom, and even the bumper stickers that encourage us to "Practice Random Acts of Kindness," agree: generosity is a gift that gives back.

Your generosity—and the time and effort it takes—makes your clients feel important.

Element Three: Sacrifice of Effort and Time

This bizarre story of the impact of exceptional client service is known worldwide. You may know it but not its entire meaning.

At 11:59 AM on October 22, 1996, a Minnesota executive appeared in the men's suits section of a store now known as Macy's. His summer weight sport coat had been promised for him at noon that day.

Because this was Minnesota, it should be stressed that the man did not need a summer weight sport coat that day and would not need one for seven months. But that promise made the client eager to pick up his coat at that moment.

The coat was not ready. Or near ready.

The man paced. It's relevant again to point out that because Minneapolis's skyway system connects most downtown buildings on their second floors, and Macy's suit department was on the second floor, the suit department was on the man's direct path to and from lunch. So he could come back for his summer coat, en route to or from lunch, on any of dozens of days over the next months.

That didn't matter. We want things on the day and time promised, even if we won't need the item for months.

The salesperson, Roger Azzam, saw the client's frustration: the client's tapping toes, pursed lips, and folded arms shouted it. Roger ran to the tailor's area and returned. Short of breath and face flushed, he told the customer, "So sorry. We will have your coat in five minutes. I promise!"

This pleasant tale now becomes remarkable.

Feeling almost embarrassed by Mr. Azzam's sacrifice—Roger still was catching his breath—the client felt obligated to respond. He spotted a dark brown wool sport coat he did not need; he rarely wore any of the seven sport coats he already had. But the man felt he needed that coat, after which he decided the coat needed a pair of black wool slacks, off-white dress shirt, and tie to go with it.

In today's dollars, his bill came to over $1,100.

People tell this story as a classic example of the Reciprocity Principle. We feel obligated to reciprocate favors. But we often respond not merely in kind but with far more generosity than we were shown.

You may be skeptical. These stories have a way of becoming urban legends, exaggerated to make them more entertaining. But the man did pay over $1,100. I know.

I kept the receipt.

The classic customer service story usually makes a nice story, but we never hear the rest. Did that outstanding service generate anything more than goodwill? This one did—over $1,100 more.

This also illustrates again one of the four keys to extraordinary relationships: generosity. We regard as our true friends those people who are generous with their time, thought, effort, or money.

Roger was generous with his effort. And for that ninety-second jog, he got $220 in commission, a lifetime fan, and a nice advertisement for his employer.

Sacrificing pays—sometimes, a lot.

The Four Acts of Sacrifice

There's the time you take, for example, to drive to and from a store to pick out a gift. Or to hand-address an envelope and handwrite the short note inside.

Those are gifts of your time.

There's the gesture that reflects a special understanding of a person, like my friend Susan Culligan, who once bought me a megaphone in my college team's colors to cheer at games, three monogrammed handkerchiefs to cry in when we lose, a large bar of chocolate to munch when the game makes me nervous, and a hip flask the width of my entire hip to carry whatever courage I might need for the big games.

That's the gift of mental effort.

It's the Nordstrom employee who steers through forty minutes of rush-hour traffic to deliver her client some cuff links for his formal dinner that night. Or the celebrated story of the Morton's employee who drove out to the Newark airport with a four-course steak dinner for a valued client. Or it's Roger Azzam risking a major coronary episode just to get me my sport coat.

That's the gift of physical effort.

Or it's the small gift. It costs you time and money. (Better yet, give your best clients occasional discounts.)

It's the gift of money, spent or given.

The gifts of time, effort—mental and physical—and money represent the four acts of generosity.

The more you spend on these, the more valued the client will feel. Because most people are driven by the need to reciprocate kindnesses, these clients will be compelled to reciprocate. Some will feel more inclined to mention you to a friend.

Merely performing the work is not enough. We need to do more. Among other benefits, these acts of generosity protect us from our inevitable mistakes. To err is human, but the client with whom we have been generous will be far more willing to forgive.

No sacrifices, no strong relationship.

Element Four: Consistency—The Follow-Up

The executives of BellSouth invited me to solve a puzzle.

They employed two huge banks of telephone support staff. After more than eighteen months, the executives noticed a pronounced pattern: their clients appreciated the service that Group A provided but *loved* the service supported by Group B. Group B's satisfaction scores were 35 percent higher.

Why, the executives wondered? The women and men in each group had received the same training and were equal in years of experience. I flew to their offices in Georgia.

On arrival, I requested the procedures manuals and all memos or emails specifying how to conduct support calls and handle customer complaints. I begin searching through the haystack and a needle jumped out of it.

It was a memo to the support team from the head of Group B:

Within 24 hours of each call, call the client and ask if his or her questions were answered and/or the problem was addressed. Note the file that you have made the call and record the client's response to it.

Group A did not receive that instruction. And that was the only difference in the policies and practices of the two groups. Group B's simple follow-up call within twenty-four hours made all the difference—a 35 percent difference.

This makes perfect sense if you understand the Peak End Rule. Group B's clients were more satisfied than Group A's because of that End: the thoughtful and prompt follow-up call designed to make sure that BellSouth had addressed the caller's problem. Group B didn't have to make that call; few services do. But that End made all the difference.

Always follow up within twenty-four hours with a simple message. "Have I answered your problem? Is there more I might do?" It makes a client feel what every client should feel: important.

Follow up within twenty-four hours, always.

An Important Sacrifice: Service Recovery

Perhaps the most vivid impact of the Peak End Rule applies to what has been called "Service Recovery."

Service Recovery is a fancy expression for "Fixing Foul-Ups." You make a mistake—you omit a patient's needed drug for treatment, charge $14 for a $4 glass of wine, or omit the client's phone number from his business cards. Now what?

We've already seen a classic example: Roger Azzam. His store botched the service initially, by failing to have my sport coat at the time promised. Roger wouldn't let it go. He raced back to the tailor and then back to me, arriving with a face so flushed and the arteries in his temples pulsing so visibly I feared the imminence of what cardiologists euphemistically refer to as "a major coronary event." Roger not only fixed my problem; he risked his life for my silly sport coat.

He made a classic "Service Recovery." And in doing it, he perfectly illustrated what two professors have dubbed "the Service Recovery Paradox." A client is satisfied with good service. But if you deliver a flawed service but fix your mistake, as Roger did, brilliantly—you "recover" from the mistake—your client ends up more satisfied than if you'd gotten it right the first time. And, in my case, he buys over a thousand dollars' worth of clothes he did not need.

How can you benefit from this paradox?

Leap into action—literally, as Roger did. At the very least, your leap conveys the key message, "You are very important to me."

Recover spectacularly. The client will remember the spectacular recovery and forget the mistake that made it necessary.

Nipping Service Recovery in the Bud

But second, focus on prevention rather than a cure so you can nip an issue immediately. Survey all of your clients with two questions and a heartfelt thanks for their responses:

1. On a scale of one to ten, how would you rate our service? (If you are spectacular, at least two people will write "Eleven.")
2. What might we/I do better?

This survey will do two things.

It will show you what to improve.

But more critically, it will cause your clients to think better of you.

I learned this from the first client satisfaction survey I oversaw for a client. Three of my clients returned their answers with a response like this one:

"I'm impressed by the fact you care enough to ask me. Very few companies do."

To protect against the need for Service Recoveries, ask your experts: your clients.

The Simplest Sacrifice

Several times a year:

Say PM, Deliver AM.

The Incredible Force of Speed as a Sacrifice

I once participated in a very revealing survey. A large research firm was commissioned to survey the clients of the five largest law firms in Chicago and Minneapolis.

Their goal was to answer the question for which every service provider would love the answer.

Why do you continue to do business with your attorney?

The survey asked the clients to rank the importance, in that decision, of over twenty-five different attributes of the attorney and firm, including credentials, fees, technical competence, intelligence, diligence, reputation in the professoion, helpfulness of staff, and the attorney's honesty and integrity.

Of the almost thirty different attributes, the clients ranked technical competence a distant eighth. It almost always is simply assumed.

Fees ranked ninth.

What ranked first? "The attorney's clear commitment to establishing an effective long-term relationship."

And what was second?

"The speed with which the attorney returns my phone calls."

That was second? That was surprising. The researchers drilled down and followed up with those who ranked speed of return first or second. They asked, "Does the attorney have to have the answer to your question, or immediate need, when the attorney returns your call?"

Overwhelmingly, the clients said no.

Then why is the speed of the return call so important?

"Because it shows that I, and my business, are important to him or her."

We crave feeling valued. We want to feel important to others. It tells us we are connected, and connection is why we are here.

Reply quickly. Sacrificing your time makes clients feel important.

Element Five: Affirmations

In 1992, a University of Washington psychology professor named John Gottman announced a discovery that would inspire his peers, fifteen years later, to name him one of the quarter-century's ten most influential therapists.

His subject, if you are the glass-half-full type, was marriage. If your glass is half-empty, his subject was divorce. And the subject of his inquiry was The Question:

Why do some marriages flourish and others fail?

We knew the old husbands' tales on that subject. The couples fight over finances and the toilet seat's habit of leaving itself up. And they fight so often and so hard that they finally exhaust themselves into and out of therapy and into court.

But Gottman's three-year study of fifty-two couples found that happily married couples fought as often and as hard as others. And the happy spouses didn't, as another old tale insisted, share more interests in common. In fact, all that distinguished the happilys from the unhappilys was a single trait.

They said more kind things about each other.

They practiced affirmations. Successful couples affirm each other five times as often as they criticize.

That, quite simply, was it.

In 2005, the law firm of Sullivan & Cromwell ranked 155th in *American Lawyer*'s annual survey of associate satisfaction. Unfortunately for the partners, the survey covered only 160 firms. Over the next nine years, the firm jumped up 85 places in those ratings. What happened in between? Seeing this result—and their 31 percent annual turnover among associates, as contrasted with the average 2.6 percent employee turnover in *Fortune*'s 100 Best Companies to Work For—the firm partners instituted a training program to encourage partners to express more appreciation.

Sullivan & Cromwell began practicing affirmations.

(A former S&C associate once described this to me more vividly: "They stopped treating us like crap.")

In 2011, the London School of Economics and Political Science published a review of over fifty studies of motivated employees. They found that motivated employees were just like happily married spouses and newly satisfied law firm associates: they worked harder when colleagues showed appreciation.

Their colleagues practiced affirmations.

In reporting this, the famous school was anticipating what Wharton professor Adam Grant, four times named that prestigious business school's number one professor, would find in his work for his bestseller, *Give and Take*:

"A sense of appreciation is the single most sustainable motivator at work."

Motivators practice affirmations.

But perhaps all the researchers should have conceded that they merely were putting numbers and new labels on what Dale Carnegie had nailed in his 1936 classic, *How to Win Friends and Influence People*:

"Nothing so inspires us as words of appreciation . . . the person to whom we have spoken them may treasure them and repeat them to themselves over a lifetime."

Nothing satisfies us more than affirmations.

Affirmations and the Knowing-Doing Gap

I know that. I know that. I know that."

Business consultants hear this every day. Their clients summoned consultants because their companies were struggling, but the consultants soon realized the company was doing just fine: it knew all these things.

It did know. But it made no difference.

Similarly, we know that affirmations work. But does that matter? In *The Gratitude Diaries*, Janice Kaplan cited a study of two thousand Americans. How were they doing at practicing affirmations? Roughly as well as Sullivan & Cromwell had been before 2005.

Only 10 percent of the people surveyed said they regularly showed their appreciation to their fellow workers.

We know that showing appreciation to our clients works. But fewer than 10 percent of the companies I've observed have thank-you programs, formal or informal.

They know but still don't do.

What is going on here? What is going on is what prompted two other consultants who heard "I know" too often—my friend Bob Sutton and his fellow Stanford professor Jeffrey Pfeffer—to publish their highly praised bestseller, *The Knowing-Doing Gap: How Smart Companies Turn Knowledge into Action*. The gap between what we know and what we do, it turns out, is as wide and long as the gulf between Cuba and Corpus Christie.

What stops us from doing? Sutton and Pfeffer uncovered several obstacles, but these three deserve special attention—including mine.

First, doing actually means just that. You have to do something, and that's work. Unless there is a clear and immediate reward for doing something, we wait until next month. And then never get around to it.

Second, some non-doers think they don't need to do something new, because they are very good at doing everything else. This is Lake Wobegon thinking; believing that all your women are strong, all your men are good-looking, and all your children are above average. It's the same kind of Kanye West thinking—the rapper/producer has compared himself to Michael Jackson, Steve Jobs, Michael Jordan, and Jesus—that prompts 93 percent of Americans to insist they are above-average drivers. There's no shortage of self-regard out there.

And third, doing—especially implementing an appreciation program of any kind—might not show immediate results, and we constantly equate a lack of immediate results with failure. None of us want to fail, and we are terrified of looking like failures. So we default to the sure and immediate wins, and postpone the rest—including the acts of affirmation that, as Dale Carnegie described so well, can last our recipients' lifetimes.

So don't just say it. Do it.

The Artist of Affirmation

The name printed on his white Disney Beach Club badge could not have been more apt. His name was Art.

For sixteen years ending on October 17, 2009, Art Lark performed—literally—as the greeter at the resort. Tall, handsome, and always smiling, Art may still be the world's only hotel greeter with a Facebook fan page and 1,691 fans.

He was unforgettable to me from the first afternoon I entered his hotel. I was pushing a stroller in which my eighteen-month-old son, Cole, was sleeping. Art greeted me as "The Gentleman" and my wife as "The Lady"—then leaned over to lift the cover of the stroller to peek at our little boy.

"Oh, God's precious little gift," Art said. Those four words all but ensured we would love our stay at the huge hotel that seemed airlifted from Newport, Rhode Island, right down to the Stormalong Bay flanking the resort—which was a sand-bottom, three-acre "pool" with its flowing river and waterfall.

Art's personal packaging alone hints at the genius of Disney. Art did not appear to be just another employee assigned to point guests to their rooms. Art was the ship's captain. He wore a perfectly tailored blue captain's blazer with a gold braided epaulet on the left shoulder, along with the pressed white slacks and white shoes that complemented the whiter-than-white gloves on each hand.

"You are so special to us," Disney seemed to convey to every guest, "that we have assigned our ship's captain to you."

But what made Art most special was Art: he glowed. And he remembered you. If you told him you were shopping for shorts that day, Art would comment on your new shorts the next time he saw you. "A *fine* choice," he would say.

We returned to the hotel three years later, this time with Cole walking alongside his tiny sister, asleep in the same stroller.

"How good to see you," Art said as we took our first steps into his lobby. As before, he leaned over to peek inside our stroller.

"Oh my, a lovely girl," he said. "God's precious little gift." I suspect even the atheists that came to the resort were touched when they heard that.

Because they understand the unique power of the first moments of the Welcome, Disney also knew the value of an Art. I've often said, "You cannot have an ordinary experience at the Beach Club after Art greets you."

The way you welcome your prospects and guests frames their entire experience with you. Disney knew that: no Florida hotel surpassed the Disney Beach Club for guest satisfaction during Art's sixteen years as its greeter.

The first act of affirmation is the warm welcome.

The Unforgettable Affirmation

Certain their C-student son would never appreciate the importance of education, my parents hatched a plan midway through my senior year: a summer-long Grand Tour of Europe. (My entire travel experience at that point consisted of two states—Oregon and Washington—and one Canadian province, British Columbia.)

They shipped me off with two instructions: "Don't call for money and come back alive." I ended up honoring one of those requests.

I met hundreds of people during those seventy-seven days in Europe, but only five I remember . . .

Bill Bradley, heading home after his Rhodes Scholarship years to become a New York Knick; Jim (I think), an engineering student from Winnipeg, Canada; Joan, a Spanish teacher in New York City; Corrina, a Swedish friend of Joan's.

And the fifth was Jim Marinelli, from Hartford, Connecticut, a club rugby player who had just completed his third year at the University of Connecticut School of Law and was planning to become a personal injury plaintiff's attorney. He drank moderately, with a strong preference for Tuborg beer.

You probably just decided, from the fact that I remember so much more about Jim, that he made the strongest impression of the five.

The truth is, I spent thirty-five days with Joan, Jim from Winnipeg, and Corrina in our car traveling through Switzerland, Italy, Spain, and France. We often took all three meals together and talked for hours on those daylong drives.

Yet the above is all I remember of those three people.

So why do I remember Jim Marinelli so well more than forty years later and the others barely at all, despite spending so much more time with them?

Because Jim had a talent everyone should develop. Roughly every ten minutes in a conversation, Jim would address me by name. "Harry, do you want to go to the Tivoli this afternoon?" Or, "Harry, what do you say we hit the disco tonight?"

No one had ever addressed me as "Harry"—other than to admonish me for something—and Jim's gesture made me feel important. And that made him unforgettable to me

It's a device that is easily dismissed yet magical. "A club should be a place," Robert Dedman, the founder of ClubCorp has said, "where the staff addresses you by name at least four times during your visit."

Why?

Because speaking another person's name—what Dale Carnegie wisely called "the most beautiful sound another person can hear"—communicates the most powerful message you can deliver to another person: "You are important to me."

Learn names and use them. (And learn all your clients' children's names, too.)

The Greatest Affirmation: Habit One

In a recent survey, more than half of all employees who had left a company gave, as their first reason, that their boss did not listen to them.

This is yet another reason to disregard the old sentiment that "imitation is the sincerest form of flattery." Imitation is the second-sincerest form of flattery; the sincerest is listening. People who truly listen to you make you feel important, and if you are experiencing that too infrequently, I recommend catching a flight to Minneapolis, which is home to two of the world's leading listeners.

The first, Stephanie Chew Grossman, is a financial service advisor with Ameriprise. She listens without interrupting, an obvious trait, but then always does something that signals she has been listening carefully and is interested. After pausing to make sure you've finished your thought, she says some version of the following:

"Now, you mentioned earlier that . . ."

Stephanie takes you back into your conversation and seeks clarification. She wants to summarize your story accurately in her mind, a desire that delivers two gratifying messages to you:

"I've heard everything you said. But I want to be sure I understand."

Notice what Stephanie does. She does not try to accelerate the conversation and get to the end; she wants you to continue. And she makes you feel that.

Stephanie's approach is one that prompted a student of listening, consultant Mark Goulston, to advise us to go beyond making those who speak to us feel they are being listened to. "Make them feel felt," he says, and Stephanie does that consistently.

Tell less, ask more.

The Great Affirmation: Habit Two

Weeks after I met Stephanie in 2014, I sensed a presence near my regular table at Starbucks. I looked up at a pretty face, warm and open.

She asked what I did every day in that seat—my answer was write this book—and we continued talking. She had written several very personal articles on healing and hoped to turn them into a book. Might I help her?

We met twice a week for almost three months. I would talk and she would listen—like no one I'd ever met. She did something I'd never seen anyone do.

She *waited*.

I'd finish a sentence, and she simply would look at me and wait. Not only did she never interrupt me; she never even interrupted my pauses after I finished a thought. She would just look me in the eyes and wait, as if to be sure I was done.

It felt charming and never got old. No one ever had made my thoughts seem so important.

Her habit reminded me of a favorite quote by the humorist Fran Lebowitz. "The opposite of talking isn't listening," Lebowitz said. "It's waiting." It's a wittier form of Stephen Covey's observation that most people do not listen with the intent to understand; they listen with the intent to reply.

This is famously true of men, of course. We don't want to be known as listeners; we want to be seen as solvers. Because of this, we think ninety seconds bemoaning a problem are more than a minute wasted. *Let's get the damn answer,* we think, *and get moving.*

But few people who request our hearing want our advice. They want our hearing. One might argue this is why most women go to hairstylists; stylists listen.

It seems a good idea to think of Lily Tomlin's advice the next time you find yourself in a conversation:

"Listen with an intensity that most people save for talking."

Wait. Several seconds.

The Affirmation and the Singing Stars

On January 31, 2012, Elizabeth Woolridge Grant, far better known as the singer Lana Del Rey, released the album *Born to Die*. It exploded on the charts. By year's end, it had sold over 3.4 million copies and reached number one in eleven different countries. Even if you have not heard of her, you may have heard her music, featured in the movies *The Great Gatsby. Maleficent,* and *Big Eyes.*

To put Del Rey's popularity in context, her four most popular songs—"Summertime Sadness," "Young and Beautiful," "Video Games," and "Born to Die"—have been heard over 410 million times on Spotify. The eight most popular Beach Boys and Rolling Stones songs—*combined*—have been heard just over half as often.

A year after Del Rey released *Born to Die*, a twenty-three-year-old, West Texas singer named Kacey Musgraves released *Same Trailer Different Park*. It eventually would be named the Grammy's and Academy of Country Artists Best Country Album of the Year. The album has sold over 510,000 copies, and her four most popular songs have attracted almost 37 million listens on Spotify—impressive, but less than one-tenth as many listens as Del Rey's top four.

And you can measure the relative popularity of those two singers by the current average price for one of their concert tickets in secondary markets: $77 for a Musgraves ticket—currently the most expensive secondary market ticket in American music—and $279 for a Del Rey ticket.

Del Rey obviously has been more successful at marketing her products, recorded music. Yet something different and revealing happens when these two singers go on tour.

In Ticketmaster's post-concert reviews by fans, 93 percent recommend Musgraves's concerts, a number barely distinguishable from the 95 percent "would recommend" scores for country music's most popular performer, Kenny Chesney. In the same Ticketmaster reviews, only 79 percent of fans recommend Del Rey's.

Is it the music? Not at all. Del Rey's smoky, three-octave contralto comes through beautifully, by all accounts. What does not come through well, it appears, is Del Rey.

"She sings her song but doesn't really connect with the audience . . . She is an amazing vocalist but had no interaction with the crowd."

And then, these three particularly revealing comments:

"She didn't even say goodbye . . . She didn't say anything at the end. Not a 'thank you' . . . When it ended, she just walked off the stage."

These comments are textbook. They illustrate the critical difference between marketing a product, such as recorded music, and a service, like a concert. *We feel about a service the way we feel about the person who provides it.* If your doctor engages you and thanks you warmly when you leave, you will remember that she performed well.

But what about Musgraves? What did she do differently? Nothing much different—until the very end. Musgraves concluded her 2015 concerts by summoning her band members to circle around her. And then they sang a cappella to their fans the warmest and most famous goodbye in country music, "Happy Trails," from Roy Rogers and Dale Evans.

Musgraves's goodbye was an affirmation. She not only was happy to have seen her fans; she looked forward to seeing them again. And took extra time and effort to express it.

And what did her customers say in their reviews?

"I felt like we were hanging out with a girl we had known all her life."

And then this telling comment:

"She had a show the next night, halfway across the country, but instead of leaving on that cold, rainy night she spent more than an hour getting personal with her fans."

Remember the Peak End Effect? It says we feel about an experience the way we felt at two points: the peak of the experience and the end. This tells us that a critical moment in any contact with a client is the very last moment: the goodbye.

End with an affirmation: master the goodbye, too.

The Problem with Attempted Affirmations

If you send every client the same annual card with a one-sentence note and your signature, the card communicates, "You are just another of my many clients."

There's a related problem with sending clients anything with your logo on it. It suggests, "Here's an advertisement for us, disguised as a gift to you. Hope your friends see it!"

And there's a third problem with these gestures. It appears they required little of your time or thought. Rather than saying to the client, "You are special," these gestures convey, "This is how much I value you. Not much."

If a client is special, make sure all of your gestures are, too.

Why the Classic Affirmation Works Better Than Ever

I once hired a designer simply because she was the first of three excellent designers I interviewed to call and thank me for considering her.

Small gestures break ties, and ties are common among services because services tend to look alike. And again, the more similar two services appear, the more important the tiniest of the differences between them.

So the findings of this survey startled me: only one in three American job applicants send thank-you notes to their interviewers, despite the fact that three of four executives consider thank-you notes in their hiring decision.

One in three job candidates send thank-yous?

Somewhere in our rush into a busier society, we have relegated thank-you notes to our bottom desk drawers, lost under our papers and envelopes.

You know this from experience.

You get your mail, only to be confronted with bills you wish you didn't have to pay and flyers for things you'd never buy.

But then, though not often enough, you get a handwritten card or note. You receive it and open it, like a gift.

You smile. You forget all those bills and pesky flyers. Someone has made your day.

When everyone sent thank-you notes, they represented winning gestures. Now that so few people do, thank-you notes represent excellent opportunities.

Be that person. Write thank-you notes.

Steps to Take Now

One: Identify Your Key Clients

You've probably heard the 80-20 rule, also known as the Pareto principle.

Twenty percent of a business's activities generate 80 percent of the revenue.

In financial services, 20 percent of the clients generate profit. The remaining 80 percent generate a loss.

Twenty percent of a business's customers make 80 percent of the complaints.

Twenty percent of the salesmen generate 80 percent of the sales.

(It applies everywhere you look, by the way. Twenty percent of the students require 80 percent of a teacher's time. Twenty percent of the fishermen catch 80 percent of the fish. And 20 percent of criminals commit 80 percent of the crimes.)

The rule applies perfectly to word of mouth, too, and my clients' most effective referring clients have three traits in common:

1. *They are extroverts.* They like people and spend lots of time with them. Clients who prefer to spend their time alone may

be profitable, but they're not good referral sources. They call on too few people.

2. *They are naturally enthusiastic.* We respond to, "You have to see Catherine, she's amazing!" We merely file away, "Catherine has done a very nice job for me." Enthusiasts tend to be extreme. Last weekend's movie was one of the best they've ever seen, or one of the worst. Referring clients tend not to live in the in-between.

3. *They're highly respected by their peers.* Most were leaders in school and currently have positions of authority. Their position and success alone make them credible to their peer group.

In short, your 20 percent are the enthusiastic people who spend a lot of time with a lot of people who trust them. These people are the medium for the most inexpensive and effective marketing you can do. Which means:

Identify these people within your current group of clients.

Who are the extroverts? Which of your clients tend to be enthusiastic? Which ones are likely to be very trusted by their peers?

If too few of your clients qualify in all three traits, choose the additional devotees from group three. While calm introverts may talk less passionately and to fewer people, those few listeners listen carefully.

Now, move to tactics. The clients who meet all three are the target of your referral strategy.

Devote special attention to thrilling each of these segments. Be particularly generous with your time and effort. Send them handwritten notes of thanks. And never communicate with them as part of a mass communication. Pull out the message and target it just to that person.

These are your devotees. For them to be most effective in recommending you, you must be specially devoted to them.

They're your Platinum Club Frequent Fliers. They get bigger seats and free scotch.

Identify your 20 percent and treat them differently.

Become the True Professional

Among the greatest compliments a service provider can receive is to be called "a true professional."

But what qualifies you for that title?

All professions—law, accounting, medicine, engineering, piloting, psychology, nursing, pharmacy, and architecture—require continuing professional education.

If you operate in a field without that requirement, you still need to learn more to perform better. Otherwise, you will simply keep repeating what you do wrong along with what you do right. You will fall prey to the problem of practice: Practice does not necessarily make perfect. Practice makes habits.

What should you do to enhance your performance?

Again, assemble an informal board of advisors of at least three people. Check in with them regularly.

If there are experts in your niche, contact them and offer them some quid pro quo for a discussion over coffee. (Three in four of these people will oblige you, not least because they valued the advice they once got and are flattered you are asking for theirs.)

Read voraciously. As one example, Walter Isaacson's biography of Steve Jobs kept me awake for nights from sheer inspiration. *Shoe Dog*, the story of Phil Knight and his famous creation of Nike, had that effect on dozens of people I've spoken with. At the beginning of my career, I interviewed sixteen successful business leaders on the books that were most helpful to them; two of them cited James Clavell's *Shogun*, a novel about political power in Japan in 1600.

Assemble a board, reach out to experts, and read.

Take a Coldhearted and Clear-Eyed Look at Your Values

I've worked with businesses of every size. The big successful ones have clearly shared values and punish and reward according to them. But this has not been true of many small businesses I've observed, and of many Businesses of One.

There are tens of thousands of small advertising agencies, for example, where if you asked, "Why are you here?" you would end up with this list:

1. Win awards.
2. Make money.
3. Still have plenty of free time.

Similarly, I have observed several startups for whom that exercise would produce this list:

1. Make a lot of money by cashing in on a market opportunity.
2. Have an exit strategy that makes us a boatload of money.
3. Have the option of not having to work again.

And I've also heard another common theme, for which you get:

1. Earn enough to be able to retire.
2. Have plenty of time for family.
3. Do work that is personally fulfilling.

All of these may be values, but none have worked in any service business I have observed. The third list, a common one, often succeeds at producing the results desired, but those results are often modest.

But one thing every thriving service business has is a list like this:

1. Make a genuine difference in people's lives.
2. Do work we truly love.

In each of the first three examples, the people came first. But in the most successful companies, making a difference in other people's lives came first.

The first group of companies are in it for themselves. The most successful groups are in it for themselves *and others*.

Which company should you be?

Advertise Your Successes

Brace yourself: this is critical.

A typical service client—yours—usually cannot tell if a service is performed exceptionally. He cannot tell if the motivational speaker left a lasting impact on his salespeople, if the tailor made the most flattering possible alterations, or the attorney won a motion that a lesser attorney would have lost. A typical service client cannot tell what is great.

But the client can know immediately that the speech went flat, that his cuffs are now an inch too short, and that the attorney lost the motion.

Few clients can tell how good they really have it—but every client knows how bad.

This leads to the cruel truth of running or marketing a service: it is much easier to fail at a service than to succeed.

To make this matter worse, most of your relationships are not deeply cultivated: a few meetings here, a lunch there. The total hours might add up to one or two dates. Unfortunately, building trust takes much longer than two dates. So any mistakes—and again, mistakes are more obvious than successes to clients—erode the client's already weak trust.

Because failures are more obvious than successes, what must you do?

Advertise your successes. Show your client what you have done. Convey the extra effort and thought.

If you beat the deadline by two days, tell her. "I know we promised this for Thursday, but I am sure you are happy to have it on your desk this morning."

If you came under your estimate by 7 percent—and do this one time in six—make sure the client knows.

If you are very proud of something, or get recognition for it, make sure the client knows.

Don't expect a client to see how hard you have worked, how much you care, or how well you have performed. A client usually cannot tell or is the last to know.

Make sure she does.

This is critical: make sure your client knows.

Alter Your Aim

I need to change my arrows. These marketing arrows aren't working."

But there's a strong chance you don't.

You may just change something else that could change your work delightfully.

A quick story behind this. I have been lucky to work with hundreds of clients I have liked, and several I love. Those people have made the difference, because you can only love your work if you love several clients and like almost all of the others.

Nothing costs you more in business, other than real estate, than a bad client. Ten percent of clients create 90 percent of the unhappiness and most of the unexpected costs. They cost businesses valued partners, key employees, and reputation.

And the too-little spoken truth is that too many providers work with too many clients they don't like.

This came home to me from a South African man who leaves no truths unspoken named Rick Mulholland. I had texted him, "What's on your mind these days? How might I help you?"

"Write about Who," he texted back from his home in South Africa.

"Who?" I answered. "Do you mean the importance of who you are, in attracting prospects and stimulating referrals?"

"No, Who you call on." And he continued with a sentence I will always remember:

"I always thought that I hated selling. But I realized I didn't. I hated the people I was selling to. So I shifted to a different market: Higher up the chain. More dollars, better clients."

Rick isn't alone. The demanding client hurts; the cruel one can flatten us for days. And we cannot blind ourselves to this: they are out there. The narcissist, the bully—like the professional golfer who has had four different caddies walk off the course in the middle of a round—the rageaholic.

Consider this response to an invoice for a complicated animation that took sixty hours to complete:

"What is this invoice? You said you charge $75 an hour. This animation is only twenty seconds long! That's forty-two cents. This is what we agreed to!"

Utterly true story.

Or there's the scope creep client who enlarges the project but expects to pay only the original fee. You don't mind the first time—those things happen. But then it happens again. And every time. It's dishonesty in the guise of just-a-bit-disorganized-at-the-time-sorry!

No.

Don't change your bow or arrow.

Aim elsewhere.

Moving up the channel works best. Most higher-ups got up there for a good reason.

It also works to move more of your marketing hours into networking. The face-to-faces also give you the chance to sample a client before you actually buy each other.

Instead of changing arrows, switch targets.

Relating: A Summary

To appreciate how the ideal provider-client relationship develops, thinking about the romantic relationship works perfectly.

First, we resist blind dates. We hate to even schedule a coffee sight-unseen. We want to know a little of what we are getting in for.

The now very rich creators of dating sites figured this out perfectly: they require that you submit a picture. And they might as well, because if you don't have a picture, no one will contact you. We need to see you; we trust our eyes, and from the photo we decide, "He looks nice. He looks like someone I might like."

You sense you might like the person—just as McKinsey's study confirmed the force of simple liking in business relationships. We only develop lasting relationships with people we like, as elusive as the idea of "liking" may be.

But we don't stop there—nor do the dating sites. They ask for a detailed profile with emphasis on hobbies and pastimes. Where did you grow up? Go to college? What is your work? And how do you play—what movies, travel, sports?

What is the site—and everyone who visits the site—trying to establish?

Again, *alikeness*. We develop relationships with people who are alike us in several ways.

What happens next? If you see someone who you think you will like, and seems like you in several ways, you schedule coffee. No obligation; you have an hour. You will see how it goes.

And what happens at coffee? You decide you like them and feel sufficiently alike, you want to see each other again, for a longer time—and a longer test of whether you might eventually enter a relationship.

You develop some comfort and perhaps the beginning of some trust. But all you really have at this point is a feeling of liking, alikeness, and some comfort.

What happens as the relationship goes on, if it develops into something beyond dating? Two things.

First, you get the *results* you want. You hoped to have some fun, good conversation, and perhaps sexual intimacy eventually, or at least confirmation of a sexual attraction. Those are the results you want, and if you both get them, you continue.

Liking, alikeness, results, and the beginnings of trust.

The parallels to a business relationship, at this stage, are clear. You meet a service-provider, you like them and feel some alikeness and comfort, and enter the relationship with sufficient confidence the provider will produce the results you want.

What deepens the couple's relationship and turns it into a committed bond?

First, you give each other time, effort, and almost certainly gifts. You make *sacrifices*.

And then you speak and act in ways that affirm your liking and, eventually, your love. You greet them warmly, speak to them appreciatively, show them they are very important to you. You offer *affirmations*.

More deeply satisfied clients, however, have an additional feeling about their provider: they feel truly important to that person. The provider creates this by making *sacrifices*—of time and effort, and sometimes financial cost. And the provider deepens this client's feeling of importance with affirmations: warm greetings and warm goodbyes, remembering their name, sending truly personal thank-you notes, and following up promptly, as BellSouth does with its Twenty-Four-Hour Follow-Up Rule.

But because good service creates the expectation of more—we humans always crave more—a provider simply must keep improving. To improve, the smartest tactic is to ask your clients: *What would be even better?*

In addition, look at your Ends: How do you end a meeting, an engagement, and the final moments of every interaction? What is your candy on your clients' pillows at the end of their long day?

If you do all of the above, referrals will follow. But you can boost your referral rate by identifying the 20 percent of your clients who are most likely to become excellent referrals.

Then, focus special attention on them. Make sure they feel very important to you. And be sure to communicate your successes to them so they will have added reason to recommend you. *You have to keep marketing, even after their business is won.*

And keep satisfying. *We always want more.*

Final Thoughts

The Final P

I found myself on a whirlwind seven-day tour of American companies several years ago—Harley Davidson, then Microsoft, then Nike. The trip then took me to Colorado for a business retreat where, on the first night, I found myself in the hotel lounge with Ian Anderson, then the CEO for Unilever Europe. Knowing Ian was a decade older and wiser than me, I knew he'd studied his company and others, and from that might be able to answer a question that my three recent visits had prompted.

And after sharing a fitting glass of Scotch—Mr. Anderson is Scottish—I told him about my three visits.

"Ian, I walked into these companies and they just felt different. I sensed it almost instantly. I could feel the fire; it was exhilarating. Is that your experience, Ian? Is that what great companies share in common?"

Ian's back straightened, his chest rose, and the color in his fair-skinned face turned a shade of flush. And he began to answer with words I still can hear, in his lovely and lilting Scottish accent:

"Absolutely, Harry. You walk into a great company, and you can feel it. The feeling is *incandescent*."

The great companies burn.

And the great people do, too.

I often saw the famous distance runner Steve Prefontaine on my afternoon runs during my last year in law school, and met him just hours after he had won yet another race—a two-miler against the Olympic gold medalist Frank Shorter.

And just hours after that—8:20 the next morning—my law review partner Jon Fusnner entered our office and yelled out to me, "You hear about Pre?'

I all but shouted back, "I did; I was there. He *beat* Frank."

"No," Jon said. "Steve died in a car accident last night."

I still shake as I write this. My ache, then and now, came from this sense: I had never met someone who was so alive, and that made his death seem so stark by contrast. I've often used just these words when I tell someone about that night and the several empty days that followed:

"Pre was so alive you could feel the heat pouring from him." The metaphor is apt: Passion burns.

If you have that fire, you will draw others to you.

It's true. The more you care, the more I will care about you. And I will trust myself in your care, whatever your care—for my business, my sore Achilles, my grieving heart.

Your passion assures me you will do all you can to help me. It tells me your work really matters, and that in the middle of some nights you will awake with an idea that might help me.

But don't ask yourself only what the world needs; merely filling some niche will never fill your soul. Instead, ask what makes you come alive. And then go and do that. Because that's what all of us need: your best you.

And so, I hope, you're now thinking, "I have that fire. Now what?"

I'd say count yourself lucky. You are at least halfway there.

And Now Where?

Your passion and curiosity have brought you this far. Now where?

Begin with the thought expressed throughout this book: Our clients today expect far more, just as we expect more of the services on which we rely. Thirty years of dramatic improvements in the quality of American products and process-based services like FedEx make people expect the same of their services.

And because your prospects see bargains and lower prices everywhere they look, they expect that quality for less. Probing for efficiencies can help you.

Because the internet teems with information—from Angi (formerly Angie's List) to Yelp—today's prospects know far more about you and your competitors. They arrive at those first prospect meetings well-armed.

Be ready. Prime that meeting and end it powerfully.

Beyond the challenges created by those changes in our lives, you face the classic challenges of marketing a service. Your prospect cannot see, test, or sample your services, because they don't exist yet, and you cannot guarantee your process because you don't have one; your work is more art than science, and to err is human. Your prospects are buying an invisible promise. In an age of mistrust, they must take your word on it, which leaves them uneasy at best.

So assure them by showing them the evidence.

But still you are selling something invisible to people who now expect higher quality, faster delivery, and lower prices than they did a decade ago, and who know more about you and their alternatives—and who worry about the ability of any service, including yours, to deliver the outcome they want.

All these challenges are enough to make you decide to go make things, instead. Selling tangible items sounds so much easier.

You're right; it is.

That's why you picked up this book—not because selling the invisible is easy, but because it is hard, and because you are willing to work hard at something you love, and because you know there is no greater triumph than succeeding at something hard. No one ever plants a flag in a tall hill.

While it's not possible to summarize all of this book's ideas for dealing with these challenges, start with these four:

Focus. Focus on a specialty that excites your passion and has an attractive future market, and become a master of that niche.

And get out there with it—with that passion. Few forces work in marketing like sheer velocity.

Focus your networking. Go where your prospects gather: trade shows, speeches, and meetings. This will bring you into contact with prospects, increase their familiarity with you, and deepen your understanding of them.

Focus your package—a truly distinctive and utterly consistent package for *everything* a prospect sees: your business card, Twitter and Facebook pages, white papers, website, everything. Your package delivers your most vivid and memorable message; make sure yours reflects how much you care.

And, not least of all, and as soft as this may sound, *keep working on you.* Character and generosity are their own rewards, but they attract others—deeper friendships, heightened self-regard, and more devoted clients.

I see this everywhere, and our world needs it: We need your very best you.

And now, thank you for coming all this way. Writing this book has been a joy and makes me feel so lucky. I hope your work brings you those feelings, too.

—*Harry Beckwith, 10/1/22*

Acknowledgments

I have two immediate debts. The first is to David Macy-Beckwith, who now has edited over eight hundred pages of my books from the kindness of his huge brotherly heart. The second is to Mel Parker, who, after publishing my first book and turning it into a worldwide bestseller, has become my diligent and devoted agent.

A special thanks to Matt Holt and his outstanding team: Brigid Pearson, Katie Dickman, Jessika Rieck, Mallory Hyde, and Kerri Stebbins.

A special line of thanks, all her own, to the utterly wonderful Shari Chistensen.

To know me is to know of my enormous gratitude for my friends. Among other gifts, they ensure that I usually hit my MacBook Pro smiling: Ryan Carrigan, Susan Culligan, Cynde Hargrave, Russ Lewellen, Megan McGregor, Becky Powell, Jim Powell, Leela Rao, and Andy Sedivy. A special thanks to Korey Derkacht, Claudia Havercroft, Cathy Phillips, Sandra Simmons, and Andrea Vincent Simonson, my friends of over five decades.

A career of gracious clients leaves me at risk of omitting one. So I will be very selective and thank Clifford Greene, whose request to address his synagogue's planning committee launched my writing career, and whose success, friendship, and counsel has delighted me for over thirty years.

And none of this would have happened without my mother, Alice, and father, Harry. In return for never making their lives easy, they made mine—a life beyond my dreams—possible.

About the Author

Harry Beckwith is recognized as the world's foremost expert on marketing and delivering a service. His clients in 21 states and on six continents have ranged from solo practitioners and venture-capitalized startups to 22 Fortune 200 companies. His 1997 classic *Selling the Invisible* is featured in *The 100 Best Business Books of All Time*, and his four other books on marketing and client relationships, translated into 23 languages, are required reading in business schools worldwide.

The very proud father of four and a Phi Beta Kappa graduate of Stanford University, Harry lives in Bend, Oregon.